Pra

"Brendan Buckley has found a gem of a story about a Vermont institution, sportswriter Dave Morse. It's impeccably researched and beautifully written, the fascinating tale of a complicated, generous and incredibly talented man who entertained his readers for decades and surely would have greatly appreciated the author's skillful writing and relentless reporting."

–Leonard Shapiro, *Washington Post*
sportswriter and the author of seven books

"Dave Morse made his living by finding and telling other people's stories. It turns out Dave had a story of his own, and Brendan Buckley takes us along on his quest to uncover and share it. His book isn't only about a legendary Vermont sportswriter—it's also an evocation of a lost age of newspapering, an uplifting account of the people who stitched a community together, and a love note to Hardwick, the town that saved Dave."

–Alex Wolff, *Sports Illustrated* writer and author of *Endpapers*

"Dave Morse's story deserves to be told. It's deeply reported and tenderly written about one of the most fascinating and interesting personalities ever in Vermont sports journalism. His life had equal moments of achievement and heartbreak and he overcame the odds to go down as one of the most caring and empathetic writers ever. Dave loved Vermont and its athletes. From high school sports to the Olympics his beat was large, Dave never big-timed anyone, and he loved skiing. His work advanced cross-country skiing greatly in my era, with his regular features of the greats of the day, and I will never forget him. His works will forever be linked to excellence and compassion in the history of Vermont sports."

–Peter Graves, ABC Sports, 1980 Olympic Games Announcer

"This is a love story between a man and a town. It is about a journalist who came to love the town of Hardwick and surrounding towns and their athletes. The love was returned many times. Dave Morse's life lives on in proud family scrapbooks and in the basketball tournament named for him that is played each year at Hazen Union High School. Poignant scenes unfold, page after page. I thought I knew Dave well. I know him even better now. And Brendan Buckley, a retired family doctor living in East Hardwick, has woven Dave's story in a readable style that makes *The Morse Code* a page turner."

—Tom Haley, the *Rutland Herald*

The Morse Code

The Morse Code

Legacy of a Vermont Sportswriter

Brendan Buckley

Rootstock Publishing

Montpelier, VT

First Printing: 2023

The Morse Code, Copyright © 2022

Release Date: August 15, 2023

Hardcover ISBN: 978-1-57869-135-7
Softcover ISBN: 978-1-57869-134-0
eBook ISBN: 978-1-57869-136-4

Published by Rootstock Publishing
an imprint of Ziggy Media LLC
32 Main Street #165
Montpelier, VT 05602 USA

www.rootstockpublishing.com

info@rootstockpublishing.com

Interior and cover design by Eddie Vincent, ENC Graphic Services
(ed.vincent@encirclepub.com)

Cover photograph by Vanessa Fournier

Author photo credit: Vanessa Fournier

Printed in the USA

For permissions or to schedule an author interview, contact the author at bbnavigator@gmail.com

For Dave's sister, Deanna French, who dearly loved her big brother, who shared my curiosity about his life's mysteries, and who was as determined as I was to see his story told.

Deanna with Dave's Vermont Sports Hall of Fame plaque.

TABLE OF CONTENTS

Foreword	By Ross Connelly	xxi
Chapter 1	TRIBUTE April 2014	1
Chapter 2	WATERBURY Dave's Childhood Years 1937-1956	9
Chapter 3	WDEV RADIO A Professional Beginning 1960-1963	25
Chapter 4	*BARRE-MONTPELIER TIMES-ARGUS* Print Journalism 1963-1965	31
Chapter 5	*RUTLAND HERALD* Professional Success 1965-1974	35
Chapter 6	CROSS-COUNTRY SKIING Shining a Light on a Sport	43
Chapter 7	MARIETTA Pianist, Singer, Bride	51
Chapter 8	THE MISSING YEARS 1974-1994	61
Chapter 9	RETURN TO VERMONT 1994	75
Chapter 10	*HARDWICK GAZETTE* A Resurrection, 1994-2015	85
Chapter 11	"THE MORSE CODE" Dave's Column	95
Chapter 12	"BE PART OF THEIR LIVES"	123
Chapter 13	MEMORIES OF UNCLE DAVE Paying It Forward	125
Chapter 14	ILLNESS AND DEATH 2014-2015	139
Chapter 15	AND IN THE END Two Photographs	143

Appendix: Dave's Appreciation Night Speech   147

Acknowledgments   149

About The Author   153

Bibliography   154

"I hope my message is clear.
Show respect of young people in particular and
it will come back to serve you well.
Be part of their lives every day."
—Dave Morse

FOREWORD

by Ross Connelly, editor and co-publisher of *Hardwick Gazette*
from 1986 to 2017

Journalism is a profession for storytellers. *The Morse Code: Legacy of a Vermont Sportswriter* is a book about a storyteller. Dave Morse was that person. He reported stories from his days as the manager of his high school sports teams in Waterbury, to his work at daily newspapers around Vermont, to his two-decade tenure as the sports editor of the weekly *Hardwick Gazette*.

His reports spawned the many stories in this short but nostalgic book by Brendan Buckley, who knew Dave well and spoke with at least a hundred people over a four-year period, asking them to share their memories of Dave.

My memory of Dave begins with a question that was pushing me to the ropes. Where was I going to find a new sportswriter? That was the recurring thought I had when Ken Burnham told me he was moving to Colorado. That was in the early 1990s, and his voice remains vivid as I think back over three decades. Ken had sold ads for the *Gazette* and was the newspaper's sportswriter. He covered the local high school teams, liked to write stories about stock car drivers from the area, and helped educate me about who the players were in Hardwick sports history. Replacing him was a task I had to do but I wasn't overly confident "replace" was possible.

Ken gave me the answer. He said he had run into a fellow who was working as a salesclerk at a Morrisville store who had covered Ken when he was a star athlete for Hardwick Academy in the early 1960s. Ken said the man, Dave Morse, had once been the sports editor at the *Rutland Herald* and before that worked at the Barre-Montpelier *Times Argus*. He said he told Dave he was leaving the *Gazette* and suggested Dave might get in touch with me to see if he could take over the sports pages.

I wasn't sure our small weekly paper would be of interest to Dave, considering his background, but I told Ken to please have him get in touch. Ken did and Dave did. He told me of his journalism background and a bit of his life, including that he left Vermont for New York City a number of years previously. He offered his life there had ups and downs but he would welcome the chance to get back into writing about sports now that he was back in Vermont.

That was the best news I could imagine. And it turned out to be a boon for readers and athletes, locally and beyond.

This book is a story about the man, his life, his family and his career as a journalist. Many of the people he covered and mentored through the years, including the 20 years he spent at the *Gazette*, fill its pages.

My memories of Dave and his writing swirl. I can see Dave sitting at his desk when I stopped into the office on a weekend, when everyone else who worked there was at home. I can see him talking with someone on Main Street, getting the details, I'm sure, for a story, the same kind of details Buckley pays attention to for this book.

It seemed Dave wrote five or six sports stories a week. I suggested he write a column and that he call it "The Morse Code." The name seemed logical to me, but he was hesitant. As with most journalists, he knew he was the news gatherer, not the newsmaker, but he agreed. The column became a must-read in Hardwick, surrounding towns, and elsewhere. Dave's musings offered opinion and memory, and often had a scoop other sportswriters around the state failed to report. This book offers a thoughtful look at those columns and lets readers see and remember Dave and his column.

I always said Dave was a walking encyclopedia of Vermont high school sports. No, better said, Vermont sports history and beyond. Uncovering surprising Vermont connections motivated Dave. If he learned about a person with one of those links, he would put words on a page so the reader learned about that person, too.

One such person grew up in San Diego, played baseball at the University of Southern California, after which he was drafted third overall in 1999 by the Detroit Tigers. He played professionally through 2010 and was a hitting coach this past season in Pittsburgh's minor league system. So, what's that have to do with Vermont sports history? A look at Wikipedia gives no indication Eric Munson had a Vermont connection. Why did he catch Dave's attention? I am a bit fuzzy about this, but a dentist in Bradford, perhaps an uncle of Munson's, was a person Dave knew. Presumably, the younger and the elder visited over the years. How Dave came across that is beyond me. Were he here, he could recount the details and make a case why Munson was a local story.

As Brendan Buckley and others tell, Dave was a regular at the Village Diner. Often, when he arrived at his desk at the *Gazette* he would say he had to get writing as he was on to another story. Most journalists would pull out their reporter's notepad (replaced today by a smartphone) and sort through their notes. If Dave's was full or he forgot it, paper napkins served him well. His desk always had a good supply, covered with his distinctive scrawl and, perhaps, a stain of food. A story always followed.

In telling various stories of athletes from area schools and beyond, *The Morse Code: Legacy of a Vermont Sportswriter* chronicles local high school history. Of more importance, though, the stories recount how much high school athletes meant to Dave and how much he meant to them.

Dave offered glimpses, well documented in this book, that let many of us know there were deep emotions within him. He let us know how important people were to him. He had empathy and that shone a light on his heart, a light that illuminated far more than game scores, player statistics, and season records.

Dave loved the kids he covered. He was quick to smile and laugh, and could also be clear when he was annoyed. He was politically astute but did not let his own leanings drift from office conversation onto the printed page. The students were his focus. I saw him cry twice in the years I worked with him. The first was when the Hazen Union Class of 2006 dedicated its yearbook to him. Those tears of joy became tears of pain in 2010 when I told him I just received a phone call that Tristan Southworth had been killed in Afghanistan. An outstanding Hazen athlete, Dave always spoke of Tristan with admiration. He respected him, I think, as much for the way he interacted with others and for wearing Number 42 on his jersey to honor Jackie Robinson as for his physical skills.

Brendan Buckley quested to dig into the sports stories that defined Dave and he found stories beyond the playing fields. *The Morse Code: Legacy of a Vermont Sportswriter* is a work that reflects the admiration so many people felt for Dave. He was a good man. It was a privilege to work with him and to get to know him. I admired him. I miss him.

Dave loved baseball. The book is a home run.

–Ross Connelly, 2022.

Chapter 1

TRIBUTE
April 2014

On a raw Northern Vermont night in February, 2014, more than two hundred sports fans headed out into the weather. They left behind their TVs, which offered highlights of the Olympic Games in Sochi, and the #8 Duke men's basketball team grinding out a 69-67 win over Maryland. Instead, the fans gathered in the Hazen Union School auditorium in Hardwick, Vermont. Aaron Hill, coach of the boys' high school basketball team, had organized the occasion. He'd invited Dave Morse, sportswriter and editor for local weekly *Hardwick Gazette,* to a team gathering ostensibly to thank Dave for his coverage of the team and particularly for his efforts to acknowledge the contributions of every player throughout the season. In truth, the event had been planned to give area athletes across all sports and their families an opportunity to express their thanks to a man whose mission over the previous twenty years had been, in his words, "to shine a light on the kids."

Dave's beat at the *Gazette* spanned as many as ten towns, none larger than 3000 people. The towns are tucked in the hills around and along the Lamoille River Valley. Many are connected by meandering, sketchily paved, or dirt roads. A one-man sports department, Dave covered a dizzying array of events across the region. A search of the *Gazette* archives yields stories covering the typical cross-section of school sports, from elementary to college. Beyond the playing fields of academe, Dave covered youth leagues, wiffleball contests, summer soccer and softball games, and snowmobile races. Farther afield, he reported from Thunder Road, a stock car track in Barre; from the Craftsbury Outdoor Center, breeding ground for national and Olympic level scullers and Nordic skiers; and from Montpelier, where the Vermont

Mountaineers, a collegiate league baseball team, summered. He drove to the top of the Appalachian Gap in the Green Mountains to witness a local cyclist compete. It was not unusual for him to travel to Dartmouth College, the University of Vermont, or other state colleges to follow homegrown athletes as they competed at the next level.

Dave's arrival at the *Gazette* had coincided with the rise of Hazen Union high school into a Division 3 boys' basketball power. From 1996 to 2010, the school had won five state championships and played in eleven final fours. In the preceding twenty-five years, the team had reached the semifinals only twice. Dave had chronicled the success of the team, as would have any good journalist. But Dave's influence across the Vermont sports world was already far greater, when he first arrived at the *Gazette*, than most people in Hardwick realized, including, in fact, Ross Connelly, the paper's owner-publisher-editor, who hired Dave.

In retrospect, it might seem surprising that a person overseeing the day-to-day operation of a Vermont newspaper would not have heard of Dave Morse. After all, he was the former sports editor of the *Rutland Herald*, Vermont's second largest paper. In that role he had traveled to the 1968 Winter Olympics in Grenoble, France to report firsthand on the performances of Vermont athletes there. He had crisscrossed New England and Upstate New York to tell of the minor league exploits of future Baseball Hall-of-Famer Carlton Fisk. He was a rare Vermont voice reporting on the creation of competitive Nordic skiing in the United States. He had moved railroad ties to help build Thunder Road in the early 1960's. Morse was even a founding member of the Vermont Sportscasters and Sportswriters Association. But Connelly had arrived in Hardwick in 1986, twelve years after Dave's last *Herald* byline appeared. Up until then, Connelly had been editor at the *Cape Cod Chronicle* in Chatham, Massachusetts. When he learned about Dave's background, Connelly worried that Dave was "out of our league," but he still felt grateful. It turned out that his worries were misplaced; the two men worked together for the next twenty years.

When he joined *The Gazette* in 1994, Dave was metaphorically emerging from the wilderness and returning to the world he had entered first as a Waterbury (Vermont) High School team manager and press liaison in the mid 1950s. In 1974, after nearly two decades of covering Vermont sports, he had abruptly, literally overnight, disappeared from the offices of *The Rutland Herald*. In the intervening twenty years there had been occasional "Dave Morse sightings," but most of the people with whom I spoke for this book, who had known Dave in previous decades, had one question in common for me:

> "What the hell happened to Dave? He vanished from the Herald; twenty years later I see him at the Aud (Barre Auditorium) writing for the Gazette!"

The tale of Dave's precocious professional success and acclaim, achieved following a childhood of emotional upheaval and tragic loss, is complicated, and until now, known only to Morse himself. It involves a fleeting love story, the demise of which triggered a breakdown; and, in turn, his years-long disappearance and isolation from friends, from family, from sports, from Vermont. He had disappeared without a word—and eventually into homelessness—before finding his way back. The years 1994 to 2014 represented a resurrection, one that he had not anticipated or planned for, one that resulted from a chance encounter, one that took place in one of the last places he might have imagined. Of the two hundred plus people in the Hazen Union auditorium that frigid February night, with two decades of shared history and conversation, only Dave knew the whole story.

In spreading the word of a budding hoops dynasty in Hardwick, Dave had tapped into his long dormant connections across the state. The news, coming from Dave Morse, carried significant weight amongst veteran Vermont sports journalists who remembered him, and so the Hazen Wildcats' star rose higher in the sky than one might have expected.

One of the speakers that evening was Brent Curtis, a play-by-play sportscaster for a radio station that broadcast local high school games. Most of those games featured smaller schools, well distant from the population hubs of Burlington and Rutland. He spoke of conversations he had through the years with other Vermont broadcasters, people who called games for the University of Vermont, Middlebury College, or the larger high schools around Burlington. He noted, "I lifted my chin, puffed out my chest and said, 'Yeah, I got Hazen basketball.'" Such was the power of Dave's reporting.

Most of the crowd in the Hazen auditorium that night hailed from Hardwick, but some had traveled from nearby towns—Craftsbury, Cabot, and Morrisville; others had come from farther away—Burlington, Fairfax, and St. Johnsbury. The prize for the longest journey went to Tim Shedd, a three-point maestro who had helped Hazen win the Vermont state basketball championship in 2000. He had traveled from North Carolina. Meanwhile, even as the evening unfolded, Shedd's former Hazen teammate, Billy Welcome, cried, stranded by winter weather at O'Hare airport in Chicago, as he realized that flight delays would prevent him from participating. He forever regrets that he didn't drive through the storm to be present for Dave.

As Dave walked in, the crowd rose to applaud. John Sperry, the athletic director, served as master of ceremonies, seating Dave next to the podium. He spoke briefly: "'Thank you' doesn't do justice for what you have done for the Hardwick community." Then he invited speakers, one by one, to share memories and appreciation. Over the next two hours, more than twenty people—parents, star athletes, second string athletes, coaches, journalists—made their way to the podium, to embrace Dave and to reflect on how Dave had touched their lives.

PHOTOGRAPH BY VANESSA FOURNIER

Dave in reporter mode at his appreciation night.

Dave Creighton, former basketball coach at Cabot High School, a tiny Division 4 school tucked in a Vermont hollow, reflected upon Dave's determination to focus attention wherever he could:

> "I want to take a moment to speak for the other towns. Thanks from the hinterlands of Cabot for all the years that you have spent on the fields, and in the gym, and for always having a moment for the coaches and the players. Dave remembers; he knows; he cares."

Billy Waller, who had coached teams at both Cabot High School and at Hazen Union, shared an anecdote that emphasized a particular feature of Dave's reporting: his determination to shine a light on all the athletes, not only the star performers. Waller recalled visiting the home of a Cabot graduate whom he had coached some years before. The home was in poor repair. Inside, the decor was bare bones, free of artwork or pictures, but several aging newspaper clippings clung to the refrigerator door. Cut from the *Hardwick Gazette*, they were copies of Dave's column, "The Morse Code", that had mentioned the boy during his high school days. "He was a substitute for our team," Waller remembered, "and yet Dave had mentioned his name in a number of stories."

Aaron Hill's younger brother, and assistant coach, Travis, had helped lead the 1996 Hazen Union basketball team to the state championship. He stepped to the podium and reminded those present about the importance of Dave's reporting locally, and of his efforts on behalf of the athletes:

> "Dave has brought that Hazen pride to our community. It wasn't there when I was little. When you put on a Hazen jersey you know Dave's got your back for life. If you lose a big game, Dave's got your back. Trouble in college? Dave's got your back. Having trouble getting a job? You know Dave's got your back. Dave, we all love you, and I hope you know that we all have your back for life."

A memorable moment, as the evening wound down, came with 2012 Hazen graduate Brittany Lumsden's presentation to Dave of a portrait she had painted of him. Twelve years younger than her brother, Randy, Brittany recalled seeing Dave at Randy's high school games, and remembered the sense of anticipation each week as the family waited to read Morse's coverage. Years later, as a Hazen athlete herself, she appreciated that one could become "famous in a small town" through the magic of Dave's reporting. She and her teammates would converge on the school library each Wednesday as the latest *Gazette* arrived. Through her brother's and her own experiences, she understood that Dave's interest went beyond the results of any one game. Reflecting on her inspiration to paint his portrait, she said:

> "He would always start a conversation with me, asking how my family was doing. I remember his enthusiasm for each player's success. I could tell that he felt like the Hazen community was his family, and I wanted to show him that we felt the same way."

Brittany Lumsden presents her portrait to Dave.

Her portrait, a head and shoulders view of Dave wearing his Hazen Union state basketball championship jacket, now hangs in the school.

No one in attendance that night knew that within only fourteen months Dave would die of an unsuspected and as yet undiagnosed illness. He was approaching 77 years of age, so perhaps people believed that he might be nearing retirement. But no one anticipated attending a standing-room-only memorial service in the school gym. Later, there was a widespread sense of solace that the community had stepped up to express its gratitude while Dave was still alive, not only for his journalism, but for so much else he had done on behalf of the community he had embraced—and which had embraced him back. "If I ever made a good decision in my life," he said to the crowd that evening, "it was coming to Hardwick."

Photograph by Vanessa Fournier

Brittany Lumsden's portrait of Dave..

Chapter 2

WATERBURY
The Childhood Years 1937-1956

Lefty Sayah's eyes welled with tears twice during my three-hour visit to his Waterbury, Vermont home, first as he described his mother's terror when, as a young woman in 1927, she stood on a bank above the swollen Mad River and cried out to her home on the other side, desperate to alert her family to the rising waters. Given the roar of the torrent, it was unlikely that her voice would have been heard. Unbeknownst to her, the family had already evacuated to ledges above the home and were safe. Still, more than ninety years after the flood, the memory of his mother being so stricken with fear brought the eighty-one-year-old man to tears. The second occasion happened as he voiced his regret for having missed out on the April, 2015, memorial service for his high school friend, Dave Morse.

Lefty and Dave were born in Waterbury, Vermont in the late 1930s. Squeezed between the Worcester Range to the east and the foothills of the Green Mountains to the west, the original Waterbury settlement grew along the Alder and Thatcher brooks. Centered around forestry and agriculture, Waterbury began to shift economically and geographically when it welcomed the Central Vermont Railroad in 1849. The train station was located a couple of miles south of Waterbury Center, and about 300 feet downhill, along the Winooski River. The gravitational pull of that hub gradually drew the town in that direction. Thereafter, most significant institutional construction took place within walking distance of the station.

A new main street sprouted shops and businesses, and the town's economy grew. The railroad opened Waterbury to the granite industry, as blocks of stone from the Barre quarries could be shipped to sheds in Waterbury for "dressing," the process of cutting, shaping and finishing the granite. In 1890, the State Hospital was built. Designed initially to alleviate overcrowding at the privately-run Vermont Asylum in Brattleboro (which housed the "criminally insane"), it became the state's primary inpatient psychiatric unit. Across the decades, its mission evolved to include care for alcoholism, depression, epilepsy and other psychiatric or chronic ailments. Dave's alma mater, Waterbury High School, opened in 1898, stood less than a mile from the train station.

Almost a century after the arrival of the railroad, the 1930s saw the introduction of skiing to Vermont. Stowe, just ten miles away, became one of Vermont's first ski areas. In the 1930s the Civilian Conservation Corps was engaged to build the first trails on Mount Mansfield. As a transportation hub, the town uncovered a new source of economic growth: tourism. "Skimeister" trains arrived from Boston and New York on winter weekends, bringing scores of tourists into the area.

The 1927 flood, so vividly recalled by Lefty Sayah through his mother's eyes, took a toll across Vermont, causing at least a hundred deaths. The Winooski River Valley suffered the hardest. Its two town centers, Montpelier and Waterbury, were devastated. The water crested in Montpelier twelve feet above street level, and the sludge left behind in Waterbury was at knee height. Before the horror of that experience had fully subsided from the town's collective memory, a second onslaught of flooding struck in 1934. In response to these events, the Army Corps of Engineers was called in to supervise the construction of a dam across the Little River, another Waterbury tributary to the Winooski. As Dave and Lefty were brought into the world, twenty-five hundred workers, again through the Civilian Conservation Corps, built the Waterbury Dam, flooding some of the land included in the original town settlement, and creating the Waterbury Reservoir. The work was completed in 1938. At the time of its construction, it was the largest earthen dam east of the Mississippi River.

Lefty grew up on a family farm in Waterbury Center, the original settlement. He was expected to be home to help with chores by mid to late afternoon. As often as he could, he timed his commute to school to coincide with one of his neighbors driving to work in the village, perhaps the town clerk, perhaps Mr. Wheeler of Wheeler Chevrolet, or Mr. Perkins. A van with bench seats served as the local school bus, but Lefty considered that mode of transportation suitable only for the younger girls. Weather was no object; "If you knew you missed 'em, you just started running," he recalled.

In contrast to the farm-driven routine of Lefty's childhood years, Dave Morse's life was marked by uncertainty, separation and tragedy. He was the eldest of four children, born between 1937 and 1943 to Hugh and Corinne Morse. Hugh's presence in the family was erratic, unpredictable, and disruptive. He was an alcoholic and a philanderer. He struggled to keep steady work. Dave's sister Deanna could recall only a four-month period of time, late in World War II, when the family of six were together, living in hired-hand quarters on a Waitsfield farm where Hugh was briefly employed, before being fired for drunkenness on the job. Even during that brief spell, Hugh would often finish his chores and head to Waterbury to see his mistress. Corinne worked as a nurse's aide a couple of hours away by train, in Brattleboro; she was regularly away for a few days at a time. It often fell to her parents and others to care for the children when Hugh was absent, which was more often than not. Unfortunately, there were periods when, often due to poor health, Morse family relatives were unable to care for the four children. During such times the children were placed in "state homes," often separate from one another.

*   *   *

Corinne's parents, Azariah (Rye) and Blanche Adams, lived about fifteen miles away in Morristown Corners. Rex and Emma Morse, who lived in Waterbury, were a second source of caregiving. Rex was Hugh's older brother. A career army officer, he had first formed (in 1936), and then headed, the local Reserve Corps, Company B. He went on to earn a Bronze Star for his service in the Pacific during World War II and retired with the rank of Colonel. In recognition of his service the Waterbury Armory now carries his name. He and Emma were childless.

Dave's father Hugh had been the youngest, by several years, of three children. Hugh's brother Rex Morse was eleven years his senior. He was raised on the Morse family's farm on Perry Hill, just outside Waterbury. Deanna remembers being told by her aunt Emma that "Gramp and Gran Morse aren't able to help look after you." The children did visit them occasionally. The elder Morses remained on Perry Hill into the 1970s.

At some point, early in her children's lives, Dave's mother Corinne contracted tuberculosis. In 1946, as her health failed, she was moved to the Washington County Sanatorium, which was located in Barre, home to the Vermont granite industry, about twenty-five miles from Waterbury. The sanatorium primarily served granite workers affected by the lung disease silicosis, which was caused by the repeated inhalation of stone dust. Those workers also suffered a higher rate of tuberculosis than people outside the granite industry. Corinne remained in the sanatorium for the last nine months of her life.

The Morse children were unable to visit their mother at the sanatorium, although Deanna remembers waving to her mother through a window from outside the building. The children knew Corinne was ill, but did not understand how imminent her death was. One evening, Dave's grandmother Blanche sat them down and explained that their mother was "pretty sick and pretty lonesome

Photograph by: Brendan Buckley

The home of Rex and Emma Morse, Waterbury, Vermont.

and wants me to come." The next morning Dave noticed her wiping her eyes and said, "Our mommy died last night, didn't she?" He was barely ten years old. His mother's obituary included the line "The children have been cared for nearly all their lives by grandparents."

Over the course of Corinne's hospitalization, Dave and his brother Don, the second oldest, were placed in a state home in Waterbury while Deanna and Dexter, the youngest, stayed with their maternal grandparents, Rye and Blanch Adams. In earlier years it had not been unusual for all four children to stay there, but, by the late 1940s, both maternal grandparents were in failing health. Following their mother's death, all four children were reunited at the Adams' home, but Rye was an invalid, and, after Blanche fell ill, her physician forbade her from caring for the children any longer.

Dave and Don returned to the state home in Waterbury Center; Deanna and Dexter were placed in Morrisville. On occasional weekends the four children were reunited at the Adams' home. On a visit to Deanna and Dexter, Blanche was so appalled at their living conditions that she appealed to Rex Morse for help. Together they decided that the two older boys would live with Rex and Emma, while Deanna and Dexter would live with Rye and Blanche, regardless of doctor's orders. Throughout his time in Hardwick, whenever Dave did reflect upon, or share glimpses into his past, he held Blanche in the highest regard, as a selfless woman who did as much as she could for Dave and his siblings in the face of her own hardships. Rex and Emma never formally adopted Dave and Don. As Emma's lifelong friend, Helen Bell, recalled, "They already had the same last name, and that's what families did in those days—they looked after their own."

Living with Rex and Emma Morse, Dave was in a stable living situation with a responsible male mentor for the first time in his life. But Deanna recalled that the Adams' home was the more nurturing environment. Rex and Emma were caring and generous, but they were more strict than, and not as warm as, Rye and Blanche. Deanna also remembered Dave as being the most sensitive of the four children and, as the eldest, perhaps the most aware of, and emotionally traumatized by, the upheaval and sadness of their early years.

Deanna pointed to a number of incidents that she recalled, or that she and Dave spoke of in later years, in which Dave seemed particularly emotionally stricken. Dave was dearly devoted to his mother. Any insult or harm to her touched him deeply. In contrast, he harbored anger towards his father throughout his life. On one occasion, while their mother was in the sanatorium, Dave arrived home from school at the family's Waterbury apartment to find his father in bed with another woman. Said Deanna, "I think that's one thing that rocked his world more than anything. It was against our mother."

Once, while Dave and Deanna were sledding together at the Waitsfield farm, they crashed and Deanna sustained a laceration near her eye from barbed wire. Dave was distraught, particularly when their father's reaction to the wound was to say, "If you don't know any better than to run into a barbed wire fence, then you deserve to have your eye cut out."

Deanna remembered Dave sobbing and clinging to grandmother Blanche's leg one Sunday, as he was being returned to foster care following their mother's death. She remembered Rye commenting to Blanche, "I don't know what's to become of that boy."

Dave was kept from his mother's funeral because the family judged him to be too emotionally fragile. He harbored resentment about that decision throughout his life. One other unpleasant memory that lingered with Dave was an occasion when his father visited the Adams' home at a time all the children were there. Due to shortage of space, Dave was forced to share a bed with his father, a man for whom he held no love or respect.

At some point following World War II, Rex confronted Hugh about his irresponsibility and drunkenness. Deanna recalled that Rex gave his younger brother three choices: to find and keep a job, to join the army, or to go to jail. By Deanna's estimate, "He didn't want to work too hard. He didn't want to go to jail. So he re-joined the army." Hugh pursued a military career into the 1960s. Deanna believes he was a medic. In the late 1950s, thinking she would enjoy living with her father, she traveled to Fort Knox, in Kentucky, to spend time with him. She had brought her prized possession, a collection of LP records. Her father threw them out. She did not stay long, and actually reported his behavior to a senior officer. "I couldn't stand it. He was drunk all the time. He went to work drunk."

In the years following Corinne's death, as long as Hugh could prove he was gainfully employed, he retained parental control, even at a distance. When Deanna was ten years old, in a mean-spirited display of parental power, and out of spite toward Rye and Blanche, he arranged for her to go into foster care in Northfield, Massachusetts. She remained there for six or seven years, with no connection to her brothers. Eventually she ran away and took a train back to Vermont. She finished high school in Morrisville, while living with Dexter at the Adams' home.

Deanna shared with me her lifelong sadness at having missed out on sharing childhood with her brothers. She was as interested as I was in learning about those years of Dave's life.

By the time that Rex and Emma agreed to foster Dave and Don, Rex had retired from the military. In 1946, he and Emma had purchased a local taxi service, which they continued to operate. Deanna remembered that they were financially better off than the Adams family. She recalls their being very social around town. "They were high-falutin," she said.

As his life became more routine and predictable, Dave came under the influence of two other men who, over the span of just a few years, would set him on a path to his life's pursuit and provide him with a moral compass.

Dave entered Waterbury High School in the fall of 1952. His years there coincided with the cross country team's run of regional dominance. In 1954, the team won the New England Championship. That high profile success attracted other boys, including Lefty Sayah, whose brother was a member of the championship team. The school principal and cross-country coach was Dascombe "Dac" Rowe. He remains a legend in the school's history, having served as principal for thirty-three years. The Waterbury town recreational fields are named in his honor.

Born in 1897 and a veteran of World War 1 who had been a German POW, Rowe was in his mid-fifties when Dave arrived at the school. Yet he remained a formidable figure – Lefty Sayah recalls a day when the team's best runner, and New England champion, Donnie Barclay, was "running his mouth and bragging pretty well." Rowe overheard the crowing and challenged his fastest runner to a race then and there. Rowe was dressed for school, down to his black low quarter shoes; Barclay was in his cross country kit, including running shoes. In Lefty's words, about two hundred yards later, "when they got up to the front of the school, neck and neck, to this day I couldn't tell you honestly which one won, but they were side by side."

Dave had come to love sports, but was not a good enough athlete to run cross country at the varsity level. As he recalled in his *Gazette* column on the occasion of Rowe's death, "After trying out for his cross country team, taking a wrong turn, and getting lost, Mr. Rowe made me his manager."

Dave went on to manage the basketball team as well. He was also responsible for calling the local AM radio station, WDEV, and area newspapers, with game scores and statistics. In Lefty's recollection, "Dave was always there to care for us. He did a good job. He didn't care if you were first or tenth, you got attention." Some years later, Dave's first steady job was as a copywriter and broadcaster at WDEV. From that beginning, he transitioned into a life of newspaper journalism.

Beyond the stability of a home and the presence of a reliable male role model, the other formative gift Rex Morse provided Dave was the opportunity to spend several weeks each summer at Camp Abnaki. Founded in 1901 as a boys' summer camp on North Hero Island in Lake Champlain, the camp served as a beacon through Dave's life.

Vermont is the only New England state without a seashore, but 120 miles, more than one half, of its western border with New York is comprised of Lake Champlain. Just ten miles north of Burlington, a one-and-a-half mile causeway connects mainland Vermont to the Lake Champlain Islands, made up of Grand Isle, North Hero, and Isle Lamotte. These islands connect to one another by bridges and extend to the Canadian border. Together they provide Vermont with 587 miles of shoreline. Surrounded by water, and with a high point of just 279 feet, the islands can feel a world apart from the rest of Vermont, the Green Mountain State. Camp Abnaki, founded early in the 20th century, sits on about sixty acres at the southern tip of North Hero Island, along "The Gut," a narrow channel that connects the northwestern portion of the lake to the broader body of water. Two large buildings, housing administration and the dining hall, sit centrally atop a grassy knoll that slopes to the water. Spread across the property are four 'villages,' each consisting of half a dozen buildings, each village serving as a home to a different age group attending the camp. Each of these housing clusters is nestled behind trees, so the view, as one stands outside the dining hall, is of acres of lawn extending down to the lake's slate-lined shore. Nothing in one's field of vision suggests that anything has changed since Dave was a camper.

The camp director through most of the 1940s and 50s was Clyde "Chief" Hess. Born in 1896, he came to Camp Abnaki having worked his entire adult life at different YMCAs in the Northeast, save for a two year stint in the United States Cavalry during World War I. On his application form for the camp directorship, Hess wrote:

> To summarize my outlook on personal religion in my life and work, I believe a YMCA Secretary has a great influence to vitalize religious views and beliefs of all classes, to be tolerant but not dormant, to be sincere but not overbearing, and to make real to those he is working with and working for a driving force for the Christian ideal of his organization.

During his tenure, he set a course aimed at tempering the competitiveness of camp activities. He was quoted in a 1954 edition of *Vermont Life* magazine (Vol. 8 No. 4):

> We do not try to turn out winners, but to have each boy excel in his own class. Where you make one winner you defeat several kids by making them feel third or fourth rate.

His goal was to mold individuals into a group that worked well together and fostered respect for every member. Campers were expected to learn to give and take in accordance with the camp motto, "Help the other fellow." From the *Vermont Life* article:

> If in a few weeks a summer camp can make a self-centered, selfish youngster into a cooperative and friendly cabin-mate, it has accomplished a high purpose.

Hess followed a similarly generous moral code. When he learned that Dave and Don (whose camp attendance was also funded by Rex Morse) had a younger brother, Dexter, whose circumstances within the Adams' home could not afford summer camp, he arranged for Dexter to attend at no cost. Ned Pike, a camper at Abnaki through the 1950s, remembers other young campers arriving at the local railroad station, "with all their worldly possessions in a box tied with string." Hess made it possible for those boys to attend as well.

Starting in 1951, while in junior high school, Dave spent several summers there, first as a camper and later as a counselor and "waterfront director." Deanna believes that her three brothers managed to avoid trouble through their teenage years because they adopted the camp's code as their own.

On the occasion of Camp Abnaki's one hundredth anniversary, in 2001, Dave compared his return to the camp with a summer weekend of baseball, his favorite of all sports, in this *Gazette* remembrance:

> As much as every game evokes memories, Camp Abnaki is more powerful to me. In 1950 I wanted to leave camp the first night. This past weekend I didn't want to go.

> They were the fabulous Fifties for me. My first job away from home, washing dishes for 350 three times a day, then becoming a counselor. Teaching Louie Washington, who gave his life in Vietnam, how to swim.

> I wrote for the Abnaki Herald back then, which has been published since "Dad" Clark founded camp in 1901, the second oldest in the country. Ken Kern chronicled our conquest of Mount Mansfield way back then, sleeping outdoors at the top of Vermont......

Bang the drums slowly, but let the roar of the
campfire, its spirit, and meaning live on!

Dave's mention of Louie Washington strikes a chord, which
echoed through his life, of respect for the military. The important
male figures of his youth shared honorable military histories. Rex
Morse had founded the local guard unit in Waterbury and fought
with it in World War II. He rose to the rank of colonel. Dac Rowe
had been a prisoner of war during World War I. Dave's choice to
mention Louie Washington in a short piece on the Camp Abnaki
reunion speaks to how deeply Dave felt a connection to those who
served our country. This theme would surface once again during his
years in Hardwick. Dave did join his friend Lefty Sayah in enlisting
in the Waterbury National Guard unit, but was medically disqualified
due to flat feet.

Dave continued to return to Camp Abnaki beyond his high school
graduation, through the late 1950s. He transitioned to the role of
counselor and waterfront director. Ned Pike, whose time at the camp
coincided with Dave's, remembered him as a kind and generous
mentor. He fondly recalled the gracious spirit that Dave brought to
his responsibilities, a demeanor that echoed that of camp director
Hess: "He was a nice person who went out of his way to help people."

Dave, and eventually his two younger brothers, formed a core of
people who helped Hess run the camp. They were there early to help
set it up, and stayed later in the summer to help close it down.

Not that Dave was a straight arrow. Classmate and eventual WDEV
colleague Brian Harwood remembers Dave hosting spin-the-bottle
parties at Rex and Emma's home after school. He remembers Dave
anxiously watching out the window for any sign of returning adults.
Lefty Sayah remembers Dave as:

> "Pretty quiet. We didn't get in any trouble together.
> Dave usually did just what he should have been
> doing. He was a good, open, honest friend. You could

say anything to him and know you weren't going to get in trouble for it. We hung out together."

Early in life Dave chose to guard against sharing much about himself, practicing a reticence around the personal that he maintained until his death. In Lefty's memory, Dave rarely spoke of family circumstances. Lefty knew Dave's younger brother Don, as he too was at Waterbury High School, "but when I heard there was a younger sister I was shocked."

Ever the willing conversationalist and skilled interviewer, Dave rarely shared insights into his own personal journey. His mother was probably his first and only constant emotional support and, even before her death, circumstances had kept them apart for significant periods of time. Poody Walsh, a sportswriter of Dave's generation who worked at small newspapers along the Connecticut River Valley, and who spent hours together in a car with him as they drove from New England to Florida one year to cover spring training, commented, "I was probably his best friend in those years, and I didn't know shit about him."

Over his twenty years in Hardwick Dave disclosed very little of his own personal history. Most of those I interviewed knew the same little pieces of information, nothing more. He would regale athletes and parents alike with chapter and verse of Vermont sports history, but rarely turn the light on himself. A line-by-line review of twenty plus years of his weekly column, "The Morse Code," uncovered innumerable tales from Vermont sports history, many of which he had witnessed, but only occasional references to his own past. As lucky as he was to fall under the guidance of academic and professional mentors and role models, it appears that Dave never found an avenue of emotional support. When overwhelmed, he turned inward and withdrew, unable to ask for help. There were several examples of such retreat and isolation during his life. He spoke to Deanna of feeling ashamed at times and, at those times, being unable to face those he knew. The sad irony of his life is that the man who was present and helpful for so many was unable to see his way to the help that others might proffer.

Living with Rex and Emma, Dave had access to more material things, but his aunt and uncle were likely not an emotionally nurturing presence in his life. Lefty's recollection of Emma and Rex is that they were quite direct, and guided Dave carefully. He remembers thinking that younger brother Don had more freedom. He described Emma as exceedingly quiet:

> "She was pretty withholding, not impolite, but she didn't say 'boo' unless somebody brought it out. I remember her sitting there staring at me, smoking like a chimney, and me wondering what she was thinking."

After school it was common for Dave and Lefty to hang out at the office of Morse Taxi, answering the phone, and sometimes heading out on runs with Doug Clifton, one of the drivers who allowed them to come along. Lefty described it as

> "Late night entertainment, hanging around there, because usually the passengers you were transporting late at night were people who came out of bars. It [sic] was quite an interesting event. A lot of them probably weren't capable of driving."

Shortly before his 1956 graduation from Waterbury High School, Dave suffered another loss when Rex died suddenly. He was just 50 years old. His obituary included an acknowledgement that he and Emma had raised Dave and Don "as their own sons since they were children."

Following his high school graduation, Dave enrolled at Burnett

Waterbury Historical Society and
Harwood Union HS.

Dave's senior year high school photo.

Business School in Boston. He left school after two years. He stayed in Boston through the summers, working in youth programs at the Huntington Avenue YMCA. He did manage through those years to maintain the appearance of a fully engaged student to Rex and Emma. Deanna is not sure whether Dave was overwhelmed by school demands or simply disinterested. She believes "that he spent most of his time elsewhere, probably at ballgames." In a 2014 column reminiscing about seeing his first major league baseball game as a high school senior, Dave owned that assessment, writing, "It was only a year or so later that I would habitat [sic] the center field bleachers at Fenway." Deanna's memory is that the school sent Dave a letter "asking him not to return."

In an October 1995 column, Dave described another extracurricular activity during those 'college' years: he helped sportscaster Ken Squier broadcast a charity event featuring the Thunder Road All-Stars at Boston Garden. Dave stayed on for the evening's main event, the hometown Celtics vs. the Philadelphia Warriors. Almost forty years later he remembered that Bill Russell set an NBA record by pulling down thirty-two rebounds in the second half, totaling forty-nine for the game. Russell's counterpart on the Warriors, Neil Johnston, could only manage four points on one for twelve shooting from the floor.

Recalling the emotional trauma that Dave had seemed so sensitive to as a child, Deanna noted his pattern of retreating, and even shutting himself off completely, from the wider world when confronted with challenges. She saw it as his response to anxiety. She believes that his experience at Burnett may have been marked by such a behavioral response. At some point, in 1958 or 1959, he returned to Waterbury. Helen Bell, who served as caregiver to Emma near the end of her life, remembers that the letter from Burnett actually went to Emma. When she confronted Dave about his truancy, he responded, "I really want to be a sportswriter." Emma took no issue with that goal, but insisted that Dave settle his accrued college debt by working for her taxi service until he had paid off the cost of tuition.

Back in Vermont, once he had repaid Emma, Dave found work at WDEV, a Waterbury-based commercial AM radio station. Over the next fifteen years, as he moved from radio into print journalism and wrote for three different Vermont newspapers, he forged a career founded on telling good stories about local events. His instincts led him to seek out stories that would resonate, not just within a town, but across Vermont. Through that work, Dave raised his profile such that, before he was thirty, with little more than a high school education, he became the sports editor of the state's second largest paper, the *Rutland Herald*. Beyond his journalism, wherever he found himself, Dave volunteered. He involved himself in mentoring youth, through coaching and administering sports leagues, and in recruiting and tutoring high school students as they served as "stringers" for his department.

Chapter 3

WDEV RADIO
A Professional Beginning, 1960-1963

In 1935, Lloyd Squier acquired WDEV, then just a fledgling local radio station. While serving as press liaison for Waterbury High School athletic teams, Dave had reported results to WDEV. Lloyd Squier became the next mentor in his life when he hired Dave as a copywriter for the station. Over the next few years Dave would progress to be an on-air voice with a daily sports report. He also teamed with other announcers to broadcast high school basketball games. Lefty Sayah stayed in touch with Dave throughout those first years following high school. He remembers him as "quiet, but did a lot of the organizing to keep things flowing....he always knew what was going on."

Squier imagined the radio station as an intimate connection to the community. His son Ken, who ran the station for decades following the elder Squier's death in 1979, recalls his father, who grew up in a newspaper family, defending his decision to buy the radio station by declaring: "More people can hear than can read." The news that mattered to listeners was local - the agricultural reports, the summer fairs that featured livestock judging, tractor pulls, and harness racing. The fortunes of Waterbury High School teams, the results of summer baseball leagues and other amateur competitions—all were of interest to WDEV's audience. Dave came to understand the importance of the local story, however small.

Dave (back row, far right) with WDEV colleagues, 1960.

In 1959, the younger Squier, who had done some announcing at area auto race tracks, was inspired to undertake construction of a speedway closer to Waterbury. Within two years a new Vermont sports venue was opened in Barre: Thunder Road International Speedbowl. Many in the WDEV family, and Waterbury at large, were drawn to the project because of Squier's involvement. Lefty Sayah bought some of the original stock at two dollars a share, and then served on one of the pit crews.

Ken Squier remembered Dave hauling railroad ties and standing them on end as a retaining wall coming out of Thunder Road's fourth turn. Sayah, who signed on with Coca Cola as a regional repairman and troubleshooter in 1961 ("If it said Coca Cola on it, it was my job to fix it"), shared a tale of the fourth turn: Coca Cola had the concession contract for the Speedway, so Sayah had a key to the track. One evening on his way home from work, in a spanking new Chevrolet

Coca Cola van, he decided to try it out on the empty track. Coming out of the fourth turn at eighty miles per hour the van slid, causing the rear bumper to strike the wall, wrenching the bumper askew. He gently backed the van into the wall so as to push the bumper back into place and returned to the company garage after hours to paint over the scrape. Such was the quality of his repair that, he said:

> "It was a month before anybody saw that ripple. By then others had used that rig. I probably didn't tell 'em for about fifteen years."

When Thunder Road opened in 1960, Dave did much of the publicity for the track, feeding reports to newspapers and other outlets. Thursday night was race night, so chosen because Thursday was payday at the granite quarries. The track opened on Tuesday nights for go-kart racing, on a separate course that wound its way through the infield of the main oval. Dave's high school classmate Brian Harwood, who was also working at WDEV and would go on to a distinguished career as a local broadcaster, recalls teaming up with Dave to participate in those races. They christened their go-kart Morsewood.

Dave's introduction to motor sports, through the construction and promotion of Thunder Road, led to his involvement in the wider Vermont world of race cars. He became the publicist for tracks across the state, including Catamount in Milton and the Devil's Speedbowl in Fair Haven. His involvement in this slice of Vermont sports continued beyond his three years at WDEV. In addition to his responsibilities at the station, he wrote for National Speed Sports News and Illustrated Speedway News.

Following his return from Boston, Dave continued his work with children, helping coach Little League and returning to Camp Abnaki for a number of summers. Phil Lovely, nicknamed Thumper by his father as a child, played baseball for the Waterbury Little League team in the early 1960's. He remembers Dave as his assistant coach, a quiet man who knew the game well. Dave kept the scorebook during their games and Phil remembers "learning a whole new language" by sitting with him on the bench.

Lovely now lives in Craftsbury. He and Dave reconnected upon Dave's moving to nearby Hardwick. Said Lovely, "It was as if nothing had changed. He called me Thumper; I called him Coach." Their reunion would have occurred more than thirty years since they sat side by side in a dugout. Yet after reporting on the exploits of hundreds of Vermont athletes over those decades, Dave remembered a childhood nickname. His powers of recall in the world of Vermont sports were described in superlatives: *legendary, encyclopedic.* It was not unusual for Dave to encounter someone about whom he had written years before and proceed to astonish that person with a chapter and verse recitation of that bygone event.

Similarly, Dave renewed acquaintance with WDEV during his tenure at the *Gazette.* The station was a regular presence at Thunder Road. The towns along Dave's beat—Wolcott, Craftsbury, Johnson—were well represented by local drivers and crew. On summer Thursday nights, Dave was trackside once again.

WDEV was also the voice of regional high school basketball. Dave Moody, now with Motor Sports Network, covered hundreds of games across northern and central Vermont. He described himself as "a one-man band—set-up, technician, announcer, color guy, statistician." Such a jack-of-all-trades performance demanded that he arrive early at the gym, often as the JV teams were playing. Dave Morse was invariably there. The two Daves would visit, sharing insights and opinions about the upcoming game. "I think Dave [Morse] would have been there anyway, whether it was his job or not. He loved it."

Moody marveled at Dave Morse's mastery of tracking both the flow and the details of a game. He imagines that Dave Morse left behind "thousands of little brown spiral notebooks" that he had worked his way through over his career. Those notebooks were filled with Dave's own version of shorthand; he would record each basket, such that he could later pinpoint a moment when the tenor of a game changed—perhaps a steal, a block, or an offensive rebound that keyed a 15-2 run. Yet somehow he also tracked statistics. Moody spoke of wishing he could have brought Dave Morse along to all his broadcasts. He described how difficult it was for him, while broadcasting, to keep track of much more than individual points, and perhaps fouls. At the Barre Auditorium, the annual site of three Vermont high school division Final Fours, he remembered that Dave was always seated in the front row of the elevated corner press box. He marveled that Dave would quietly appear at halftime and lay a sheet of paper in front of him. "I don't know how he did it, but there it was: offensive rebounds, defensive rebounds, turnovers, steals!"

Chapter 4

BARRE-MONTPELIER *TIMES-ARGUS*
Print Journalism, 1963-1965

In 1963, Dave moved full time to written journalism when he was hired by Henry Jurras, sports editor of the *Barre-Montpelier Times-Argus*. Jurras spent most of his professional lifetime at the paper. He became the next, and perhaps last, important mentor in Dave's life. In his remarks of thanks in the Hazen auditorium fifty-one years later, as he reflected on the professional path that led him to the *Hardwick Gazette*, Dave singled out the guidance and education he received from Jurras during his two and a half years working for him.

> "My first newspaper job was at the Times-Argus with the great Henry Jurras. I covered those great Spaulding teams you hear about—'62, '63, '64."

The lightning that struck with the emergence of the Hazen Union boys' basketball team late in his career echoed the feats of another Vermont high school basketball juggernaut during his first years as a print reporter. The Spaulding High School boys (of Barre, Vermont) won the state championship over four consecutive years, 1961-64. Within a year of arriving on staff at the *Times-Argus*, Dave was on the Spaulding boys' beat. Chronicling that team was a perfect ticket through which Dave introduced himself to the wider Vermont sports journalism network. He followed them to the end of their reign, with a loss to Bennington Catholic in the state championship game. As his profile grew across the guild of Vermont sportswriters, so did his professional influence—while at the *Times-Argus* he was instrumental in establishing the Vermont Sportswriters and Sportscasters Association. As he had in Waterbury, Dave again found time to participate in youth sports. He served as league administrator for both the Little League and Babe Ruth area teams.

In the early 1960s, not far from the Barre-Montpelier axis, the basketball and baseball teams of a smaller school were forging an as yet unrealized connection to Dave's future. A generation before his arrival at the *Hardwick Gazette*, a group of boys at Hardwick Academy blazed a trail of athletic success across Vermont's northern tier. While Spaulding High School held sway across the biggest, 'Class L,' schools of Vermont, Hardwick Academy, a 'Class M' school, just twenty-five miles to the north, was winning its way onto the sports pages. The Hardwick Academy Terriers, precursors to the Hazen Union Wildcats whom Dave would later cover, not only reached the Northern Vermont Basketball Finals in 1964 and 1965, but also won the baseball championship in 1964. Ken Burnham was batterymate to star sophomore pitcher Jon Dimick. He also started at forward on the basketball team. The *Times-Argus* assigned Dave to cover both those Hardwick teams. Thirty years on, Ken Burnham went shopping at Caplan's Department store in Morrisville and, while checking out his purchases, recognized the store clerk. A conversation ensued, during which Ken remarked, "Hey Dave, the *Hardwick Gazette* is looking for a sportswriter. You should go talk with Ross Connelly."

Another beat that Dave worked for the *Times Argus* was American Legion baseball. The Legion season picked up as the school year ended, and the league crowned a champion in early August. From 1964 to 1966, the Barre entry in the league won or contended for the league title and, in 1966, won the state championship. Three players from Hardwick Academy played for that team. Jon and Barry Dimick and Dave Brown regularly traveled to Barre for practices and games, sometimes hitchhiking. Their participation coincided with future Hall of Famer Carlton Fisk playing for the Bellows Falls, Vermont team. Fisk spent more time on the mound than behind the plate in those years, and usually played shortstop when he wasn't pitching. At least twice, Jon Dimick and Fisk faced off in pitching match-ups. On both occasions Bellows Falls won, in large part due to Fisk providing just enough pitching and clutch hitting. Both times Dimick was dominant, but a late inning extra-base hit by Fisk proved the difference in each game. Thirty years into the future, Dave would renew his connection to those Hardwick teammates. Meanwhile, his coverage of Fisk would continue for several more seasons, spanning Dave's tenure at three Vermont newspapers.

Jon Dimick also attracted major league scouts. Both the Orioles and the Mets expressed interest in him, but Jon's father, Wendell, drove a hard bargain, insisting that the offer include the cost of a college education. The scouts were unwilling to make such a commitment and were unable to convince Wendell to agree to their terms. The scouts walked away. Jon's teammate, Dave Brown, recalls the meeting taking place in Hartford, Vermont following one of their Legion games. He remembers Dave Morse also witnessing the negotiations. Jon was dismayed at his father's intransigence. He briefly attended the University of Miami before being drafted into the Army, and then serving in Vietnam. No other teams ever expressed interest in him.

Dave left the *Times-Argus* in the fall of 1965 to become the first head sports editor of the *Springfield Times-Reporter*, a paper in Springfield, Vermont. He covered sports along the Connecticut River Valley for only a year before taking his most significant career step when he accepted an offer to head the three-person sports department of the *Rutland Herald.*

Chapter 5

THE *RUTLAND HERALD*
Professional Success, 1965-1974

Rutland, Vermont lies just west of the Green Mountains, only about seventeen miles from the New York border to the west, and about halfway between Massachusetts to the south and Burlington, Vermont to the north. Today, it is at the crossroad of US Routes 4 (east-west) and 7 (north-south). Driving east along Route 4, the road immediately begins the climb up and over the spine of the Greens, reaching the Killington Ski Resort access road in about a dozen miles. The downtown district is immediately west of Route 7, towards Otter Creek, which meanders north another thirty miles before spilling into Lake Champlain.

As Waterbury had flourished with the arrival of the railroad in the middle of the nineteenth century, so did Rutland. It served as a crossroad for a rail line between Burlington and Boston, and another connecting to New York City. As it had in Waterbury, the introduction of rail service prompted businesses to migrate towards the railroad depot. In Rutland, this migration led somewhat west of Main Street (Route 7), resulting in the development of Merchants Row. High quality marble had been discovered in the Rutland area decades earlier, but it was only after railroad service was established that the industry grew to become one of the world's busiest marble centers. Redfield Proctor consolidated the local industry into one

giant corporation, which eventually included marble quarries in
Colorado and Alaska. In its heyday, the Vermont Marble Company
employed several thousand workers. Both the United States Supreme
Court building and the Jefferson Memorial feature Vermont marble.

By the time Dave arrived at the *Rutland Herald* in 1966, the local
granite industry had slowed. The nearby quarries had closed before
the end of the twentieth century, and the main line of the Rutland
Railroad was closed in 1961. And yet, Howard Coffin, one of Dave's
colleagues at the *Herald,* described Rutland in those years as "thriving,"
in part due to the manufacturers that operated there. General Electric
had opened a Rutland plant in 1957 to manufacture engines and
engine parts. Howe Scale Company, which made equipment to
weigh almost anything, was an internationally known manufacturer.
Other mid-century manufacturers included Tambrands and Metro
Mail. The Lincoln Iron Works produced tools and equipment for
the quarries. Rutland Fire Clay Company began as a source of clay
to repair brickwork, but evolved to making products for cleaning,
repairing and patching chimneys and furnaces. Coffin, who covered
the city, remembered there being "lots of politics, and a little bit of a
criminal element. I loved it. It was a hell of an education."

In 1965, based in a town with a population between eighteen and
nineteen thousand, the *Herald*'s circulation was about twenty-two
thousand. It was the second largest paper in Vermont, behind the
Burlington Free Press.

Kendall Wild was the managing editor. He served the paper for
forty years, starting as a reporter in 1952 and retiring in 1992 as
editorial page editor. Born in Chicago, he moved to Vermont with
his family as a child, and was educated at Rutland High School and
Harvard University. During the course of his career he mentored and
trained a core of reporters who would go on to success and acclaim at
larger publications (*Newsday,* the *St. Louis Dispatch,* the *New Yorker*),
universities (Dartmouth and the University of Vermont) and on
Capitol Hill (press secretary for Senator Jim Jeffords). He set high

expectations, modeled the determination and grittiness he expected from his charges, and fostered an esprit de corps that filled all who worked for him with a sense of pride. An example of his commitment to excellence was his traveling to North Carolina during the Civil Rights struggle of the 1960s to bring his readers a firsthand view of this important story.

Howard Coffin was hired as a city reporter in the spring of 1966, just months before Dave Morse arrived. He stayed on until 1978, before pursuing publicist work at Dartmouth and the University of Vermont, and ultimately serving Senator Jeffords. He is best known across Vermont as a leading expert on the roles Vermonters played in the Civil War. He unabashedly remembers the *Herald* of the 1960s and 70s as "the best small town paper in the country." Although he and Dave worked different beats, they shared a love of sports and often attended games together. Occasionally Coffin would serve as a stringer for Dave if he needed additional reporters to cover a full slate of weekend games.

Reminiscing about Dave, decades after they worked together, Coffin recalled that he and Dave initially bonded over their love of sport. They often dined together and invariably talked sports, not politics, art, or literature. Coffin's respect for Dave was great: "He was smart; he had a quick mind. He was a good sportswriter and a good editor, and he knew sports."

A particular memory Coffin shared that spoke to Dave's perceptiveness around sports harkened back to a winter night in the early 1970s. Coffin was working late when Dave burst into the newsroom, raced to Coffin's desk and exclaimed, "I've just seen the best basketball player to ever play in the state of Vermont!"

"Whoa," Coffin had replied, "remember that Bob Cousy and Bill Russell have both played in the Rutland High School gym when the Celtics have played exhibition games."

"I know," Dave had said, "but this kid is the best ever!"

Who had so impressed him that evening? It was Julius Erving, playing for the University of Massachusetts. "And, you know," said Coffin, "maybe Dave was right!"

Both Coffin and Dave's fellow sportswriter, Ted Ryan, remember that Dave would occasionally disappear without notice. Coffin expressed amazement that Wild tolerated the absences, but sees that tolerance as evidence of the enormous respect he had for Dave. Coffin does not doubt that Wild "was pissed, and would give Dave a piece of his mind when Dave returned." but noted that Wild also quietly stepped in to fill Dave's role during those times. Ryan recalls that Dave's unscheduled departures occurred mostly around the transition from winter to spring, when the sports calendar was relatively light. His memory is that Dave traveled to spring training, and, not unusually, overstayed his time away. Ryan was not especially troubled by Dave's eccentricity and simply took on what extra work was demanded until Dave returned.

> "Working so closely with Dave over a decade, I realized he had his own struggles and challenges, even though I didn't always know the details. Most of the time when he was 'AWOL', it was in the spring. I didn't care and didn't bother management about it."

As they worked together, Dave and Ryan's relationship evolved to suit their strengths. Ryan recalls Dave as the more outgoing of the two.

> "He was gregarious. He knew everybody; he knew every rumor, knew everything that happened. As sports editor, he became hugely prominent in the community, really well respected, and I think, well loved. His presence in the community was his strength, his ability to forge relationships."

Ryan saw himself as more conservative, more office-centered, more concerned with the details of the day-to-day coverage. In describing their work patterns, Ryan expressed no frustration or rancor. He felt great admiration for Dave.

> "We had a really good rapport. I can't remember a time we clashed in any sense. It was fun. We both worked extremely hard. I always thought Dave and I had complementary skills. In my opinion, that made us the best sports coverage team in Vermont."

The respect that Dave achieved in the wider community was mirrored at the *Herald*. Ryan and Coffin both attest to that, and to managing editor Wild's appreciation for Dave's work. In contrast to his "gregariousness" in the community, Dave's leadership style was quieter, and always supportive. Through the years he mentored several students from local high schools and colleges who expressed an interest in journalism. Many went on to successful writing careers across the state. Ted Ryan was one of those mentees, initially stringing for the *Herald* while a senior at Rutland High School and then commuting sixty miles from the University of Vermont to report when he could through the late 1960s. Ryan describes Dave's editorial style as:

> "Quiet, helpful and never condescending. He was never one for glory. He got his points across that he needed to get across. I learned a lot about sports writing from Dave in terms of developing my own style. I don't think I realized his effect until later."

Mike Donoghue grew up in Burlington and started interning at the *Burlington Free Press* while still in high school in the late 1960s. A rivalry existed between the *Free Press* and the *Herald*, but the sports departments cooperated with each other to share scores and stories from their respective ends of the state, so Donoghue knew Dave even before he chose to attend St. Joseph's College in southern Vermont. While pursuing his degree, he did some stringing for Dave, primarily covering high school sports in the towns of Bennington and Arlington. Donoghue did not own a car; his primary mode of transport was hitchhiking. He remembers that it was not unusual for Dave to offer to pick him up from events. After his graduation, Donoghue returned to Burlington and a career with the *Free Press*. Decades later, when Dave came to the *Hardwick Gazette*, they became reacquainted and developed a strong friendship. Donoghue's obituary of Dave appeared in the *Gazette* and other papers around Vermont.

Tom Haley was drawn to a career in sports journalism from his exposure to Dave's reporting. While a student at nearby Castleton State College, he served as Sports Information Director. They traveled together to Connecticut one year when Castleton played an NAIA baseball tournament game there. Haley says:

> "Riding down there that day with him was a thrill, an absolute thrill because I always read him. I loved to read what he wrote."

He describes "turning cartwheels" when he learned that Dave was back in Vermont, covering sports for the *Gazette*.

Mike Rosenberg, class of 1967 at Rutland High School, interned at the *Rutland Herald* during his senior year. He describes Dave as ensuring that Rosenberg would have events to cover. He appreciated that Dave "made us feel as if we were doing something important. He knew that high school sports matter to a community." He remembers Dave as "a great teacher; he corrected me in such a gentle way." Rosenberg went on to a career as Metro editor for the *Lowell* (MA) *Sun*. He reconnected with Dave years later, when Dave was at the *Gazette*. Reflecting on Dave's connection to community

Rosenberg observed, "In Hardwick, Dave was doing just as he did in Rutland, but in spades."

As remembered by his colleagues and mentees, Dave had a remarkable equanimity while overseeing a busy sports schedule at a newspaper that demanded excellence. Howard Coffin reflected that it was only after Dave left the *Herald* that he became most aware of this enviable quality:

> "When Dave was working the desk on a busy sports day the pace could be frantic, with the phone ringing endlessly as stringers called in their stories. As the calls came in, Dave would pick up his extension without fanfare and take down the story. [Dave's] calm stood in stark contrast to the man who replaced him: each time he was alerted to another incoming call, he would let loose with a litany of oaths and sputtering. It gave me a new appreciation for how Dave had managed his job."

Coffin remembers that Dave kept sports in perspective, and that, used properly, sports could reveal the fundamental goodness of human beings. Mark Candon, a 1970 graduate of nearby Proctor High School, a small school sports super-power in Vermont, recalled that, following a playoff soccer game, he and some teammates visited Dave at the *Herald* office that evening to look at photos from the match. Dave expressed frustration that the best action shot failed to include the ball. With a smile, he proceeded to cut out a ball from a separate print and superimposed it onto the preferred picture. It was featured in his story the next day, with 1970s-era "photo-shopping!"

Coffin provided a lovely tribute to the man he shared so much time with across eight years:

> "He wasn't one of those fans who went panting after the athletes. He understood sports; he understood

what they were about, and he understood the
goodness in them. I had the impression from him,
in all the hundreds of games we saw, that we were
enjoying not just a sporting event, but a human
experience. He was a level above most sportswriters.
He was an extraordinary person."

Chapter 6

CROSS-COUNTRY SKIING
Shining a Light on a Sport

The Putney School, a private high school in Putney, Vermont, sits in the Connecticut River Valley, across the state from Rutland. It is not possible to travel east-west across Vermont along any route remotely approaching a straight line, as the Green Mountains form a north-south spine down the length of the state. The distance between the offices of the *Rutland Herald* and The Putney School is about sixty-seven miles; the travel time in good weather, about ninety minutes. In winter, it all depends.

John Caldwell taught math at the school and coached cross-country skiing. He had been a member of the 1952 United States Olympic Ski Team, competing in the combined event, a test of cross-country skiing and ski jumping. He coached a number of future Olympians at the school and went on to coach several Olympic teams, including 1968 and 1972, when Dave Morse worked at the *Herald*. Additionally, Caldwell was instrumental in forming the first US Nordic Womens' team to compete in the Olympics, which was in 1972, in Sapporo, Japan. Martha Rockwell, whom Caldwell had coached at Putney, headed up that first team of women.

Until Bill Koch's remarkable silver medal finish in the 30 kilometer event at the 1976 Innsbruck, Austria Olympic Games, Nordic skiing occupied a sports backwater in the United States. In southern

Vermont, John Caldwell was slowly building a foundation for the program, but he hardly garnered headlines.

Peter Graves grew up in Bennington, Vermont, where he was coached in Nordic skiing by Bucky Broomhall. Broomhall came from US Nordic skiing royalty, as his older brother, Chummy, had competed in the Olympics and went on to be responsible for course maintenance at the Squaw Valley (1960) and Lake Placid (1980) Winter Olympics. Bucky Broomhall twice led Western State College to the national skiing championship. Along the east-west axis of route 9 that connects Bennington with Brattleboro, close by Putney, there was excitement that a new breeding ground for top flight skiers was developing.

Graves made the Junior National team and attracted interest from colleges. He chose to head west to Fort Lewis College in Colorado. After competing for Fort Lewis, he spent his career in broadcasting and announcing, serving as a TV analyst at Winter Olympics and as a public address announcer at high-level national and regional cross-country ski events across the country. As a prominent figure in Vermont sports, he was invited to the Vermont Principals' Association Hall of Fame ceremony in 2013. He recalled being seated next to an elderly gentleman and introducing himself.

"Yes, I know who you are," the man replied. I used to cover you in competition. I'm Dave Morse."

Remembers Graves:

> "It was a powerful moment. He was a hero of mine. I got up and gave him a hug. I remembered a quote from my ski coach, 'Peter, your heart is smiling.' It was true that night. I said to Dave, 'You did so much and here tonight maybe not everybody remembers, but I remember, and thank you.' That was very, very powerful, because I didn't know if I would see this guy again. That was very important to me."

Graves cried as he recalled Dave's coverage of Nordic skiing during those heady days in southern Vermont, as Caldwell and Broomhall nurtured a growing force of top athletes.

> "If you were anywhere in southern Vermont, you read The Herald. It was a prestigious family-owned newspaper. It became a regular go-to for this high school kid, and that was driven by the coverage of Dave. He cared about the athletes. He cared about the words he chose. He tried to put the best possible face on American cross-country skiing. I was an early fan of Dave Morse, long before I ever met him."

John Caldwell set up a series of night cross country ski races, held at different locales under the lights. Dave Morse traveled across the winter landscape to cover those events. Graves described him as "the only source" for news of cross-country skiing.

> "Dave realized what these Vermont athletes were doing— and he appreciated the work ethic and the passion, that this was a very tough sport. He helped create a sense that Vermont was at the forefront, centered around Putney."

Dave's pride in the contribution of Vermont athletes to the nation and to the world dated back to his early love of sport. He recalled the Winter Olympics of 1952:

> "I would rush to Vincent's Pharmacy in the morning to read about Andrea (Mead) Lawrence of Rutland, who won two gold medals. There it all was in the results page of the newspaper."

During a time he was playing a role in divulging the news of his high school's sporting results, he was acutely aware of the excitement experienced by the receiver of such news. Years later, he still considered Andrea Mead Lawrence to be Vermont's greatest athlete.

In the summer of 1969, John Caldwell arranged for his skiers to hike the length of the Long Trail, a 272-mile footpath along the Green Mountains that stretches from Massachusetts to Canada. It is the oldest long distance hiking trail in the United States. Graves accompanied the hikers for one section of the expedition. Then still in high school, he remembered, "I was with my heroes, and Dave covered every step of that thing."

During the winter Nordic racing season, Dave's reporting included regular updates from Europe. He would supplement the wire copy with his own prose, "the AP with Dave Morse," Graves said. "For me, he was ahead of his time."

A recollection by John Caldwell reinforces that opinion. He wrote to me of:

> An interesting event in the early years. We had a national ski championship meet at the school. Meanwhile, Brattleboro High School had a basketball game. In the next day's Brattleboro Reformer (less than fifteen miles from Putney) the sports section had no mention of the ski meet. I knew the editor, John Hooper, and wrote or called him to ask what the hell was going on with the sports section. Meanwhile, some guy I never heard of named Dave Morse is calling me from Rutland to ask me for results and comments. It was enlightening, and Dave continued with his coverage through the years. I'm sure he had a good effect on the development of XC skiing in Vermont. Good for him. He saw the big picture, the chance for development.

As Peter Graves' skiing improved, Dave wrote stories noting his progress. "It was like being anointed by the king," recalled Graves.

In 1968, Dave Morse was the only Vermont newspaperman to travel to Grenoble to cover the Winter Olympics. Of the twenty-two athletes named to the US Alpine and Nordic ski teams that year, eight hailed from Vermont. Over the two week span of the Olympiad, Dave wrote several stories, primarily focusing his attention on the Vermonters, allowing wire reports to provide the event highlights. Former *Herald* colleague Tom Haley recalls a story Dave wrote about local alpine skier Harry 'Rebel' Ryan. Appropriately nicknamed, Ryan invited Dave to accompany him on a drive through the mid-winter French Alps in his newly acquired Porsche. Dave wrote that as they "sped back to the Olympic Village, Ryan showed adept reflexes at avoiding a speeding French-driven (sic) minibus."

The US Nordic Team entered Grenoble with high hopes. Dave wrote that Mike Gallagher, the best US hope for a medal, believed that it was "the best ever time for US cross-country skiing." However, 22nd place (50K) and a 27th place (30K) individual finishes by Gallagher were the best the US could muster, while the relay team finished in twelfth place. A couple of Dave's stories made note of the strong connection to US coach John Caldwell and the burgeoning development of Nordic skiers across southern Vermont.

The champion and local hero of those Olympics was Jean-Claude Killy, who won gold in all three Alpine events. In a deliciously tongue-in-cheek front-page *Rutland Herald* story under the headline "Uh, Pardonnez Moi....," Dave described his fruitless effort to score a one-on-one interview with the superstar. He was one of two English speaking reporters in a press phalanx that descended upon "the French encampment." From the article:

> After numerous false alarms, 'Le Superman' appeared. He was quickly surrounded by French radiomen, while others with tape recorders thrust boom mikes towards him ... our chance seemed

near at hand since we knew the national hero speaks
English. We edged in and asked if he would answer
some questions. He brushed away and dashed back
to his room.

Oh well.

Dave may have been known for occasional prolonged absences
from work, but he was hardly one to shirk his responsibilities. His
last story from Grenoble, which appeared in the February 20th
edition, covered the bobsled event. On the 21st, pictures of local high
school basketball appeared on the sports page, taken by Dave. And a
couple days later, he covered a collegiate skiing competition from the
Middlebury College Snow Bowl.

Years later, while Dave was writing for the *Hardwick Gazette*,
another opportunity to cover Nordic skiing came his way. The
Craftsbury Outdoor Center, just fifteen miles away, was becoming
a new training ground for young Vermont skiers. On the grounds of
the former Cutler Academy, Russell and Janet Spring had created
a recreational hub, based primarily on Nordic skiing and summer
soccer camps. Over time, they expanded to include runners' camps
and sculling on adjacent Big Hosmer Pond. Their emphasis was to
create a facility that encouraged easy and inexpensive access for all. The
accommodations, which were based in the old school dormitory, were
simple, but the food was renowned for its excellence. John Brodhead
joined as director of skiing in 1981 and created programs for youth and
adults. He also founded the annual Craftsbury Ski Marathon, which
quickly became a must-do event for skiers nationwide. Gradually, the
Center's reputation and influence grew.

Fluky winter weather is not unusual in the northeast; occasionally
it leads to snow-dependent events being forced to change locale
on short notice. And, if Dartmouth doesn't have snow, it is likely
that Williams and Middlebury are more brown than white as well.
Craftsbury is tucked into the hills of Vermont's Northeast Kingdom

(Caledonia, Orleans, and Essex counties), far from the modifying effect of Lake Champlain. In 1997, as other parts of New England experienced thaws and rain, Craftsbury was spared. So it was that the NCAA asked, on fairly short notice, to move its championship Nordic races to that venue from the originally scheduled site of Trapp's Outdoor Center in Stowe. A reunion of sorts occurred as Ken Squier, Lloyd's son, and by then a nationally known figure through his reporting of NASCAR events on CBS, brought WDEV on site to broadcast from Craftsbury. Of course, Dave was there too.

I was a spectator there that weekend. I had only just begun to know Dave, as he was a regular presence at the youth events in which my children competed. I had yet to learn his history and thus I fell prey to assumptions: as I watched him roam about the grounds of the Outdoor Center, small spiral notebook and pencil in hand, I wondered at how this small-town reporter was taking to such a national-scale event, writing about a sport that he had never covered before......foolish me.

Over the next seventeen years, Dave reported on activities at the Center and on the 2008 transfer of its ownership to Dick Dreissegacker and Judy Geer. Former Olympic rowers, they had once served as sculling coaches for the Spring family. Their vision was similar to the Springs': to create and manage a recreational center that afforded access to all, especially the local population. Neither family had an interest in an upscale resort. The emphasis would remain on the activities, which Dick and Judy would build upon. They attracted new coaches, expanded the capacity, and formed the Green Racing Project, a program that sponsors recent college graduates to pursue their training. In return, the athletes serve as youth coaches across all age levels.

Today, many collegiate ski team rosters feature the names of Craftsbury Outdoor Center alumni. Hannah and Emily Dreissegacker, Susan Dunklee, and Ida Sargent, all of whom had learned to ski and train in youth programs at the Outdoor Center, represented the

United States at either or both the Sochi Winter Games of 2014 and the PyeongChang Winter Games of 2018. Hannah and Emily's mother, Judy Geer, recalls that:

> "Dave came to EVERY high school or other ski event that he could, and was always so interested in how all the kids were doing, and so excited for them, and so eager to share their successes and their stories."

Ida Sargent's father, Dave, echoed Judy Geer's observation, remembering how impressed he was that Dave seemed to know the names of all the children competing, not just the Olympic hopefuls. Sargent also worried that, on some occasions, Dave was not dressed warmly enough, but that he never retreated from the cold.

Chapter 7

MARIETTA
Pianist, Singer, Bride

Marietta Burns, who would later marry Dave Morse, was born in Wyoming, Ohio, outside Cincinnati, in either 1932 or '33. The handwritten page in the 1940 US Census that includes her family describes her as the seven-year-old middle child of Hordie and Nahlia Burns. Hordie was listed as a "truck driver, general hauling," having earned $600 over forty weeks of work in 1939. Marietta was Black, but all those with whom I spoke, who knew Marietta as an adult, described her as fair-complexioned. Her daughter-in-law, Barbara Munlin, told me she believed that Marietta could have passed for a white woman.

In February 1949, Marietta, then a 16-year-old high school junior, and Willie Clifford Munlin, age 20, applied for a marriage license. He listed his profession as "horse trainer." Later that year, Marietta gave birth to a son, William Loyd Munlin. The birth of a second son, Win, followed in 1950. Marietta attended Wyoming High School, but probably did not graduate. Her picture appears in the Junior Year class photo of 1949, but not in the 1950 edition. Marietta had an affinity for music, as a pianist and singer. At some point, while her children were still young, she moved east to pursue a career as a nightclub performer. Her sons were raised primarily by their paternal grandparents, Otis and Melinda, but Marietta did not forget her children. Barbara Munlin (William's widow) recalls her bringing them out to stay with her in Maine on occasion during the summer months. Barbara did not know of her marriage to Dave Morse, but when told of it, responded, "Likely she was after his money."

Marietta's obituary describes her as "an accomplished musician" who had performed in New York City. I found a two-line notice from the "Cabaret Tonight" listings in the October 29th, 1962 edition of the *New York Times*:

> Cafe Leon, 67 West 44th Street, Marietta Munlin, singer-pianist.

This was several years before she would have met Dave. I was unable to track down any recordings, although Carol Levesque, a stepdaughter, remembers having her records in their home. At some point in the 1960s or early 1970s she established a recurring gig in the Pheasant Lounge of the Bardwell Hotel, a block from the offices of the *Rutland Herald*. Dave met her there, perhaps as early as 1969.

Ross Connelly remembers Dave sharing his love of jazz. Brian McCarthy, Hazen Union class of 1998, has forged a career at the forefront of the Vermont jazz scene. He remembers Dave expressing interest in his career, and greatly appreciating that McCarthy would give him new CDs as he released them. Similarly, Tommy Gardner, who reported for the *Gazette* from 2008 to 2013, recalls Dave's love of jazz. He spoke to Tommy of living in New York, and of having easy access to great music. When and where did Dave develop his love of jazz? Was it through Marietta, or was it the passion he developed for that music genre that then led him to discover her? Is it possible that his appreciation had been forged much earlier, through exposure to Ken Squier's evening jazz program titled "The Cave of the Winds" on WDEV radio?

Poody Walsh, who spent several days with Dave as they traveled to cover Major League Baseball spring training in March 1969, remembers him talking on the phone to "a black woman" from their motel room. On consecutive nights Walsh witnessed Dave sobbing on the phone as he tried to convince the woman not to leave him. Poody felt badly about witnessing the scene. Yet, for all the hours they passed together in the car, Walsh never felt he knew Dave well.

> "He was a very private person, not revealing at all. I knew he had attached himself to a lady who didn't want much to do with him, a Black singer. He embarrassed the hell out of me telling her how much he loved her and all this stuff. She had apparently broken off the relationship. He was appealing to get her back."

Walsh seemed confident that the woman was the same person whom Dave did eventually marry in 1973.

Through those years, when Walsh was writing for the *Claremont* (New Hampshire) *Eagle Times* and Dave was at the *Herald*, they were the best of friends. "I would go to Rutland a lot. We'd always sit together. He never talked about this lady." Walsh cannot imagine that anyone else was as close to Dave as he was, and yet he said, "I don't think he had close friends. I don't think he attached himself to anybody."

Ted Ryan, who joined the *Rutland Herald* sports staff full time in 1969 after stringing for years, first as a high school student in Rutland and then while a student at the University of Vermont, remembers Dave telling him about a singer at The Bardwell Hotel.

"I began to hear more and more about her, and one day he asked me to go over with him after work so he could introduce me to her."

Ryan's custom was to head home to his family after work, but he could tell that this woman was very important to Dave, so one day he agreed to go. Ryan has only vague memories of Marietta. In fact, due to the dim lighting when they were introduced he was not aware she was a black woman. He recalls harboring concerns for Dave when he learned that Dave and Marietta were engaged.

"She was an entertainer. As an entertainer she's not going to stay in Rutland. Sure enough, she moved on to other places."

Others at the paper shared his concerns. He remembers one of the managing editors commenting, "Dave's in love, but she's in love with weddings."

Dave's sister Deanna brought her family to the wedding, but no other Morse relatives chose to go. In Deanna's mind, there was clear disapproval of his marrying a Black woman. Deanna's son, Aaron, who would have been a young boy at the time, describes Marietta as "stunningly beautiful and classy." No one else from Dave's circle of family and friends with whom I spoke could tell me anything about Marietta. Rutland was far away from Dave's immediate family, and Dave was too busy to return home very frequently. It seems unlikely that he ever brought Marietta north from Rutland.

A fuller picture emerges from two other sources: Mara Meehan, who, at age nine or ten, served as ring bearer for Dave and Marietta; and Carol Levesque, Marietta's step-daughter from her subsequent marriage to Lewis Atwood in Maine.

Meehan (nee Horwitz) grew up outside of Philadelphia. Her neighbors were Bill and Lenora Brooks. She believes that Marietta was their niece, and a regular visitor to the Brooks' home. As a young girl she was very taken with Marietta, "I loved Marietta. She was a larger than life figure" who made her living as a singer and pianist. She remembers her delight at all of Marietta's "fabulous costumes." Meehan's mother was a skilled seamstress, so she often went next door to help Lenora with the repair and tailoring of Marietta's outfits. The accessories, long necklaces and feather boas, also captured Mara's fancy. She describes Marietta as having a somewhat husky, deeper voice, and "she smoked like a chimney." Occasionally Marietta would perform. Her repertoire included love songs and jazz standards. She accompanied herself on the piano.

Meehan thinks she might have met "Mr. Morse" when he visited next door, but isn't sure. Marietta asked Meehan's mother to serve as her matron-of-honor at the wedding. It followed that Meehan and her younger brother served as flower girl and ring bearer, respectively. Meehan remembers driving "for what felt like a week" to reach Rutland. She remembers rehearsing her role and being nervous before the ceremony.

The ceremony was held in Rutland's Unitarian Universalist Church on November 17, 1973. As Dave and Marietta walked back down the aisle, the assembled serenaded them with a rendition of Take Me Out to the Ballgame. Deanna remembers chairs being pushed against the walls, and a wild dance party ensuing. Sadly, Dave's aunt, Emma Morse, chose not to attend the wedding. Deanna believed that she did not approve of the interracial union. She remained a champion in Dave's eyes, but her absence that day must have pained him.

The marriage lasted less than a year.

Carol Levesque was a middle-school aged girl in Maine when her father, Lewis Atwood, married Marietta, in November 1974, only weeks after Marietta had obtained a divorce from Dave in Bath, Maine. The marriage to Dave had lasted just over forty-eight weeks. Levesque believes her father and Marietta had been dating for about a year before they married.

What did Dave and Marietta share over those forty-eight weeks?
Between their two schedules of games and gigs, how much time
were they together? What was Marietta thinking? Was she a
heartless gold digger who thought she had found a wealthy man?
Dave dressed well and drove a nice car. Was she taken in by those
trappings? From the reports of his *Rutland Herald* colleagues, Dave
was smitten. How painful to imagine if that affection flowed in only
one direction. Is it any wonder that the sensitive boy who had lost
his mother grew up to become the man devastated by the collapse
of his marriage?

In answer to a question about her understanding of Marietta's
life leading up to the marriage with her father, Carol Levesque
responded,

> "Her life before my dad I don't know anything about,
> except I knew that she had the sons, and we met
> them once or twice. I think she was probably very
> private."

Over the next eight years, Carol knew Marietta as 'Netta,' who:

> "Always had projects for us, crafty sorts of things,
> or cooking plans. We made meatballs once; she gave
> us the meat and all the spices and watched us do
> terrible things to ground beef."

She described Marietta as:

> "Extremely talented. She decorated like Martha
> Stewart; she made wedding gowns in her fabric
> shop (the Thread-Needle Shop in Bath); she was a
> gourmet cook; she had two or three jazz albums."

Mara Meehan does not believe she saw Marietta again after her marriage to Dave. Levesque was unaware of a prior, recently ended, marriage before her father wed Marietta.

What happened? Dave shared with his sister Deanna that the greatest disappointment and embarrassment of his life was his inability to keep the marriage together. He did not share with her any further details of their struggles. No one I spoke to, many of whom knew Dave very well, possessed any knowledge or insight into his relationship with Marietta.

Dave's first column after his wedding appeared on Thanksgiving Day, November 22, 1973. He made no mention of his nuptials.

In the fall of 1974, Dave covered Middlebury College football while Ted Ryan covered the University of Vermont. Ryan remembers Dave being excited when Middlebury was scheduled to play one of the Maine schools because it would give him a chance to see Marietta, as she was performing there. It was his recollection that he never saw Dave at the *Herald* again, but history suggests something different must have unfolded.

The only Maine school on Middlebury's schedule that season was an away game versus Colby on September 21st. Dave's coverage of that game, and the next weekend's contest, Middlebury at home against Wesleyan, appeared in the paper. His last column for the paper was written for the Monday September 30th edition, with his byline and "Herald Sports Editor." The following weekend Middlebury played home versus Worcester Polytechnic Institute. Dave did not cover the game. By October 18th, Ted Ryan's articles included the designation "Herald Sports Editor."

Here is how Ryan recalls events: he received a phone call late one Sunday evening from the editor-in-chief asking him who was putting the sports together for the Monday edition. (At the time the *Herald* did not publish a Sunday paper, so the Monday sports section included all the weekend action). Ryan replied that it was Dave's turn to do the Sunday duty. "Well, it's dark over there," he remembers being told. He assumed that Dave had forgotten the schedule and so he went in to do the job. "Dave never returned; I never heard from him. I didn't want to become sports editor that way."

Such a clear memory of a Sunday night call to work must be accurate; I believe it was not the weekend Dave traveled to Maine, but one of the following two Sundays. I think Dave must have seen Marietta while covering Middlebury in Maine on September 21st and learned catastrophic news — that she was in love with another man and wanted a divorce. Dave managed to hold himself together over the next week or two before breaking down and abandoning Rutland. Ted Ryan remembers that the *Herald* office was able to track Dave's movements for a while, as he put charges on the office credit card. Dave's habits were such that it was not entirely unusual for him to disappear from work for several days, but never during a busy time of year. Ryan did his best to cover for Dave over the next two weeks, until one morning he was confronted by the managing editor, point blank, "Where's Dave?" Unable to answer, Ryan admitted he did not know. "OK, that's it. He's done."

Ryan remembers that Dave had been under considerable stress for a couple of reasons. Sadly, he had become a target for racist hate mail and calls following his marriage. Marietta's travels also put a strain on him. Ryan only learned later that Dave had been sleeping at the office for some time before he finally left. Was he planning to move elsewhere? To rejoin Marietta?

Ryan remained at the *Herald* until 1975. He never heard from Dave again while there. He remembers Deanna calling him to learn if he knew where she could reach Dave. No one seemed to know where he was. After Dave returned to Vermont many years later, Ryan saw him from time to time. On reflection, Ryan continues to have great affection for the man who mentored him from high school through college and then as a colleague. His sentiments, below, echo Deanna's experience of Dave in times of stress.

"There were so many good times early, and then some sad times. He could disappear so thoroughly you couldn't even reach out to him."

And:

"It wasn't just a case of Dave being Dave, but feeling for him and his problems. Never a minute I would want to give back from my time working with Dave."

Chapter 8

THE MISSING YEARS
1974-1994

I doubt that anyone but Dave Morse himself has a clear idea of how Dave passed the next two decades. None of the nearly one hundred people I interviewed for this book were able to provide me with a reliable chronology as to where he was or what he was doing.

Former colleagues and family members glimpsed him from time to time, but none who asked questions came away with answers. Dave dropped some hints, but hardly enough to allow me to bring those years fully into focus.

Outside of a well-documented brief return to Vermont, the common denominator for peoples' memories, for Dave Morse "sightings," and for Dave's own shared glimpses into those years is the New York metropolitan area, either in the city proper, or in nearby communities along the Hudson River Valley. Undoubtedly he spent some of that time in the world of public relations, but there are some who think he may have found his way back to sports, or at least to journalism. For a time, he clearly did well. He dressed nicely, drove a good car, and shared money with nieces and nephews. It is also without question that Dave fell on extremely difficult times — low paying jobs, destitution, perhaps homelessness. Remaining much less clear is the timing of, or an explanation for, those peaks and valleys.

Through my interviews, it became clear that Dave was a master of deflection. As artfully as he plumbed the thoughts of an athlete, coach, or administrator, so did he guard against revealing his own secrets.

Opportunities to reveal himself did arise. Dave loved conversation; it was a life skill that he had honed. Whether in his office at the *Gazette*, in a booth at the Hardwick Village Restaurant, or sharing a table at Connie's Kitchen, Dave filled his days with talk.

Lynn Delaricheliere became a co-owner of Hardwick's Village Restaurant in 2013. She found herself there most days, as she oversaw its refurbishing and day-to-day operations. She remembers Dave being there every day. "He'd come in around 10. Sometimes he'd have a sandwich, sometimes blueberry pancakes. Once in a while, he'd mix it up and have some toast." He always sat in a booth by a window overlooking the Lamoille River. He would position himself so that he could look across the room and watch the front door to see who came in. Once seated, "He was like a magnet, an absolute magnet. If you could have fit ten people in that booth, there would have been ten people sitting there!"

On quiet days, he sat alone at the booth, writing in his ever-present spiral pocket notepad. He would still "talk up a storm" with the wait-staff. Occasionally Lynn or one of the others would sit with him to chat, but on most days, "there were three hundred other people there first."

Lynn's husband, John Sperry, was the Hazen Union Athletic Director. Before taking on ownership of the restaurant, Lynn had only known Dave through his high school sports coverage. At the restaurant, she came to know him on a much more personal level, perhaps as well as anyone in Hardwick. But she too could sense the walls that Dave put up to shield himself from divulging much about his years away from Vermont. She recalled:

> "He talked about New York City - 'I kind of traveled
> ... ,' and the conversation would stop there. I tried to
> break through, but he would steer the conversation

towards (his sister) Deanna. We'd start talking about when they were kids and were separated. He felt, as a child, that he needed to figure things out for himself, and that he needed to make sure the other kids (his three younger siblings) were taken care of. In those recountings, his grandmother Adams was a pillar of greatness."

He spoke with Lynn of his marriage, but barely revealed a glimpse. Lynn recalls him telling her, "It didn't last very long. We were different people doing different things." Said Lynn:

> "I kinda let it go. If he had wanted to say anything else ... and, if you pushed him too hard, there was that shut-down. There was all truth to it, but he only shared so much. When he talked about his life, what was left out was left out very intentionally."

No one I spoke with ever found Dave to be rude in conversations that touched on his life story, but many people described a sense of a boundary that they seemed to understand should not be breached. From the people who knew him best, I heard variations on the same story: he was briefly married to a Black musician; she left to pursue her career; he lived in New York City for some years. That was it.

Dave's return to the world of Vermont journalism led to his rekindling friendships with colleagues he had worked with in the 1960s and 1970s. When I spoke with them, many wondered where he had disappeared to for so long. Fellow journalists, they were surely skilled at asking questions, yet none had managed to breach Dave's defenses to learn about his life during those twenty years away.

Over his two decades in Hardwick, Dave Morse forged many new friendships and reconnected with athletes whose stories he had told thirty years before. None ever learned very much about the years leading up to his arrival there.

I fault myself. I came to know Dave pretty well through his tenure at the *Gazette* up until his death. He had been the *Rutland Herald* sports editor during my undergraduate years at Middlebury College. We knew athletes in common from those years. His *Gazette* beat found him covering my children as they grew from their elementary school introductions to sports to their participation at the collegiate level. How had I failed to not know him better? Shortly after his death, I was visiting with his sister Deanna. "You know," she said, "we lost Dave for several years." I was dumbfounded. From that moment, I have tried to follow his trail through those years, but it quickly turns cold, and the clues are few.

I know that some of his colleagues from the past suspected that those years had been marked by emotional pain, particularly as his initial disappearance from the *Herald* was so clearly triggered by Marietta's departure. Perhaps this awareness discouraged them from asking many questions. One day, as Dave and I discussed the fallout from a racially charged incident at a local school, he casually mentioned that he had at one time been married to a Black woman. My instinct was to politely acknowledge the fact, but not pursue it. It was tangential to our conversation and, I thought, perhaps too emotionally charged to explore. That was all I ever heard from him about Marietta.

Lynn Delaricheliere remembers him admitting to her that he struggled with depression. He described to her a "need to be hidden. 'I don't want to be seen.'" Surely that description matches certain moments in his life: his not returning to Vermont after failing school in Boston, his disappearance from Rutland, his disappearance from family, his occasional "walkabouts" from his journalist duties at both the *Herald* and the *Gazette*, as recalled by Tim Ryan, Howard Coffin, and Ross Connelly. His sister Deanna remembers Dave describing to her his overwhelming sense of shame at having failed at marriage.

Comparing himself to his siblings, he told Deanna, "You and Dexter kept your families together. I couldn't even keep a wife." It makes sense that he could not imagine facing his *Herald* colleagues, so many of whom had attended his wedding. And so he left.

Others had gleaned similar tidbits from his biography. Several with whom I spoke knew of his marriage to "a Black singer." More than one understood that she had left him "to pursue her musical career." Some knew that he had spent time in New York City. They wondered if he had pursued Marietta there, but it seems that she settled in Bath, Maine for the rest of her life. Ross Connelly remembered how moved Dave had been by his encounter in New York City with Rachel Robinson, widow of Jackie.

I combed through twenty years of his *Gazette* stories. Occasionally, he would drop in a memory or anecdote from his past, mostly from his youth. I did learn a little bit, but barely enough to sketch out (emphasis on "sketch") his path from October 1974 to April 1994.

October 1974

In the days and weeks following Dave's disappearance from the *Rutland Herald*, Ted Ryan recalls that the editors were able to track Dave's whereabouts because he continued to charge expenses to the *Herald*. Ted remembers Detroit and Toronto appearing on the account. Was Marietta performing in those cities, pursued by her distraught husband?

Across the next two decades, I can occasionally locate Dave in time and place with some confidence. Aside from a few months in Vermont, and occasional visits back to family there, each sighting takes place in New York City. I believe that, for better or for worse, from October 1974 until early 1994, that is where he lived, worked and, sadly, struggled.

January 1976

When Ted Ryan moved from the *Rutland Herald* to the *Burlington*

Free Press, he picked up a plum assignment, University of Vermont (UVM) men's hockey. UVM had made the leap from Division 2 to Division 1, from the world of small colleges to that of the larger eastern universities and college hockey powers. The Eastern Collegiate Athletic Conference held an annual holiday tournament at Madison Square Garden in early January. UVM was invited to participate in 1976. As Ted sat watching a UVM practice session, a voice hailed him from behind. To his surprise, there stood Dave. "He materialized out of nowhere. It was such a shock." Ted learned that Dave's work involved writing about lumberjacks, but was not clear as to who employed him. Was it a chainsaw company? A PR firm? A lumberjack association? In a *Hardwick Gazette* column decades later, while discussing a lumberjack program training course being held at the Green Mountain Tech Training Center, Dave wrote:

> It's something I was actually familiar with, with the Homelite Tournament of Kings a while back.

That tournament, the International Chainsaw Cutting Championship, was first held in 1978, "billed as the lumberjacks' Super Bowl, the World Series of chainsawing" (*New York Times*, Sept. 23, 1979).

Ted described Dave as "looking pretty good, but there wasn't the glint in his eye that he had in Rutland, or that I saw again when he came to the *Gazette*." Ted reminded Dave that many people in Vermont asked after Dave and cared about him. Ted encouraged him to return.

March-August 1976

Deanna recalled quite specifically that Dave had been back in Vermont "when the Charlemont Restaurant burned." The Charlemont was in Morrisville, near where Deanna lived. Her memory was that Dave had covered the event for the local weekly paper, the *News and*

Citizen, but his byline does not appear in that publication's coverage of the story.

Ted Ryan was certain that he had employed Dave as a stringer for the *Burlington Free Press*. As he recalled, Dave was back in Vermont, "within a couple of years, max." In fact, the *Free Press* coverage of the Charlemont fire carried Dave's byline, April 24, 1976. Deanna had the right event, wrong publication. What had led to Dave's sudden return to Vermont when he appeared to be doing well in New York just months before? Perhaps because their interactions with Dave were infrequent, family members struggled to place their memories in a clear chronology. Deanna shared a memory of Dave being in debt due to an accumulation of speeding tickets and parking violations: "He was a careless driver." Might that be a reason he returned to Vermont in 1976?

Over the next few months, Dave's byline appeared several times in the *Free Press*, mostly in the sports pages. He covered high school basketball; Burke Mountain Academy, an emerging ski school; a cycling road race; the Burlington International Games (an annual youth multi-sport event between Burlington, Vermont and Burlington, Ontario, held that year in Ontario); a Vermont-New Hampshire high school all-star soccer exhibition; and the American Legion baseball tournament.

Remembers Ryan, "Then, it kind of happened again, where he sort of disappeared. I don't know at all what ever happened. I remember his sister calling me again. Apparently he had her car, so I knew he'd gone off the radar again."

Deanna's son, Aaron, recalls that Dave stayed at his family's home for a time during Aaron's childhood. He specifically remembers that one of his brothers had to give up his room so that Dave had a room of his own. He too remembers being aware that his uncle struggled with debt and "uninsured cars." His mother spoke with him about Dave's struggles with depression. I believe Aaron's memories coincide with these months in 1976 when Dave was back in Vermont.

1976–1980-something

Deanna's recollection of the period when Dave was completely lost to the family was that it spanned a period of seven or eight years, ending when he returned to Vermont for good in 1994. Her son Aaron moved to Massachusetts in 1989 and returned to Vermont well after Dave had himself returned. Aaron remembers that, during his time in Massachusetts, his mother reported to him during phone calls that she had not heard from Dave in a long time, and that she was worried about his mental health. Therefore, Dave must have maintained some connection to his family until the mid to late 1980s. Working on that assumption, from the time of his second sudden disappearance in 1976 until the mid to late 1980s, Dave must have visited the French family from time to time. He was not one to call home, or provide advance notice; he would simply appear, usually around a Thanksgiving or Christmas holiday.

Aaron's recollection of visits from Uncle Dave are happy ones. He drove a nice car, wore nice clothes, and handed out $50 bills to him and his four siblings. They loved those visits, "We were always excited to see him, as he was attentive to all five of us." Aaron remembers at least a couple of such visits from Dave.

Another person who remembers visits from Dave is Helen Bell. She and her husband lived in the upstairs apartment of Emma Morse's Waterbury home. Emma's husband, Rex, had died many years before. She and the Bells became close friends, and so the Bells came to know Dave well through his visits to Emma whenever he was back in Vermont. Dave endeared himself to them during those visits. Helen related how important Dave's emotional support was to her in the wake of Emma's 1997 death. She described his being present for her as "invaluable" through that time. Interestingly, she remembers that Dave always referred to Emma, who had taken him and Don in after their mother died, as "Mamma."

Across these years, three work scenarios emerge from people's recollections of Dave: first, his coverage of lumberjack events; second, reporting for a town newspaper somewhere along the Hudson River, north of New York City; third, working in a coffee shop in New York, where he met Rachel Robinson. Finally, and likely coinciding with his absence even from his family, Dave had a period of destitution, perhaps homelessness, before returning to Vermont in 1994. Deanna also believed that Dave might have been hospitalized in New York for treatment of his depression.

Deanna remembers that he occasionally traveled out west to cover lumberjack competitions. I believe he attended (and perhaps wrote about?) these events as an employee of Mekler-Ansell, a Madison Avenue public relations company that counted the Homelite Corporation, manufacturer of chainsaws, among its clients. In his *Gazette* article discussing the lumberjack training program, Dave wrote:

> Such shows are found from Bangor, Maine to Susanville, California, with stops in Hayward, Wisconsin; Old Forge, New York; Albany, Oregon; Altoona, Pennsylvania, Prineville and Kalispell, Montana." Perhaps he listed those towns from memory of another time?

In a May 2013 column Dave reviewed the movie "42," the story of Jackie Robinson. Robinson was one of Dave's favorite players, if not absolute favorite. At the close of the column, he provided a glimpse into his years away from Vermont.

> Having taken an 'extra' day job while working for Mekler-Ansell in New York, I waited on the gracious and petite Mrs. Robinson and daughter at a deli on 57th Street.

Mekler-Ansell was founded in 1968. Its offices were at Madison

Avenue and 40th Street in New York City. Dave shared with Ross Connelly that he had traveled the country covering lumberjack events. The January 1976 copy of *Chainsaw Age Magazine*, a trade publication, covered the opening of Homelite's new company headquarters in Charlotte, North Carolina. An accompanying photo shows a representative of Mekler-Ansell Associates interviewing Homelite's president, Franklin Atwater.

Assuming that Dave was working for Mekler-Ansell when he surprised Ted Ryan in early 1976, did he return to work for the company again, after disappearing from Vermont for a second time? Connelly remembers that Dave held Leonard Ansell in high regard. They shared a love of sports. Given that the first Homelite Tournament of Kings took place in 1978, and assuming that Dave's knowledge of the event was through his own experience, then it seems likely that his tenure at Mekler-Ansell would have included a stint that included some of the late 1970s and/or early 1980s.

Another memory that Ross Connelly shared from his conversations with Dave is that there was a time when Dave pursued purchasing a 'chain of weekly papers.' Ross believes that they were based somewhere north of New York City, along the Hudson. Dave told Ross that he had approached his aunt Emma, in the hopes that she would front him the money, but she declined. Helen Bell also remembers when Dave asked Emma for the loan. She notes that Emma's rationale for turning him down was that, "It's better if people go to the bank for money, not to their family." Mike Donahue remembers Monticello, New York, a town in the Catskills about a hundred miles from the city, somehow figuring into Dave's life. Perhaps Dave had found a journalism job there? Might this fit with another nephew's memory from 1982?

September 1982

David French, another of Deanna's sons, was en route home to Vermont while on leave from the Navy. He spent a day touring the city with his uncle. Dave met him at Grand Central Station and brought him to several tourist locations: the Battery, the Empire State Building, and St. Patrick's Cathedral. They visited an "Irish Sports Bar" near the Port Authority Bus Terminal, from which French caught the bus home. Recalls French:

> "Everyone in the sports bar seemed to know Uncle Dave. They brought him a coffee, asked me what I wanted. Everything was sports for Uncle Dave. He seemed fine, in good spirits."

They did not visit Dave's workplace or where he lived. French's recollection is that "he was writing sports for someone." He also thinks that it was not long after their visit together that his uncle "went underground."

Brendan Greene, a Hazen Union basketball alumnus, confirmed that Dave might indeed have spent some time covering sports while in the New York City area. Greene had forged a close rapport with Dave during his high school years. He was one of a number of boys whom Dave helped to attend summer basketball camps, through financial contributions and by aiding in transportation. On one occasion, Dave volunteered to drive Brendan back home from a Five-Star camp held at Fordham University. During the drive, Dave reflected on his time living in the metropolitan area, and spoke of the thrill of attending an event at Madison Square Garden with a press pass. I was not able to find any record of his work as a print journalist during these years, but the possibility does dovetail with his reported interest in purchasing the newspaper group.

Will Voigt was a multi- sport star at Cabot High School before playing soccer at Pomona College. He has spent his career as a professional basketball coach both in the United States and abroad. He knew Dave while in high school, and again later when he coached the Vermont Frost Heaves of the semi-professional American

Basketball Association. He, too, recalled Dave speaking of covering sports in New York City, "not at all boasting, just, oh, by the way."

May 22, 1990

In a September 2008 column that included other baseball memories, Dave wrote that he attended the White Sox-Yankees game at Yankee Stadium on this day. He vividly recalled the game because it was the occasion of Carlton Fisk taking Deion Sanders to task at home plate for disrespecting the game by not giving his full effort. Dave's account includes two intriguing references: first, "having lived in the city for twelve years," and another phrase acknowledging that his apartment building had a doorman.

Does the "twelve years" reference 1978-1990, or 1982-1994? If Dave resided in a building with a doorman, he was on solid financial footing, at least in 1990, but that was not to last.

Both Tom Haley and Howard Coffin, colleagues of Dave from his *Rutland Herald* years, related stories of a *Herald* staffer unexpectedly encountering Dave in New York. Haley's version was that Dave was behind the counter "in a sandwich shop." Coffin's anecdote is grimmer, as Dave was seen in a state of relative destitution on a New York corner. "He was clearly a homeless person. It was very sad." Neither Haley nor Coffin could place either event accurately in time, nor did they identify the *Herald* staffer behind the story. Each gave me several names to try, but each lead proved incorrect.

Undoubtedly Dave fell on very hard times. Was his taking on work in a coffee shop the start of his world unraveling? Did Mekler-Ansell have insufficient work to keep him employed?

Throughout his life, when challenged, Dave would disappear. Was there a health or emotional crisis during his years in New York that prompted him to disappear and then lose his job? That would mesh with the possibility that Dave was hospitalized at some point during these years.

During this period, Deanna hired a private investigator to look for her brother. She phoned hospitals in New York City to inquire whether her brother was a patient there, perhaps unable to speak for himself due to illness or injury. Bellevue Hospital responded by asking her to visit the hospital as they did indeed have an unidentified patient. Deanna, heart in her throat, made the trip to New York. The patient was not her brother.

She called homeless shelters. She learned of a Dave Morris who had recently stayed at one of the shelters she called. She wondered if Dave had altered his last name, out of embarrassment, or to avoid being found. Beyond knowing that Dave had been living and working around New York City, she had little to go on. No lead bore fruit. The years passed without word from, or news of, Dave.

Chapter 9

RETURN TO VERMONT
1994

A good family friend, who had grown up and gone to school with Dave's siblings, Dexter and Deanna, worked in local law enforcement. He often spoke with Deanna and understood the degree to which she suffered emotionally from not knowing where Dave was. Unbeknownst to Deanna, he successfully located Dave through a system intended for use only in tracking down criminals. Deanna believed he did so through Dave's social-security number, and she has chosen not to mention the officer's name. "He stands next to God in my judgment," she said. "He cared about how much I was suffering and decided to help."

One day in early 1994, the officer called her at work. He told her he had located Dave, that he was alive, employed and safe. "Go home. I think he will call you." Deanna raced home and indeed Dave called. She wept and implored him to come home. And he did.

"He came with the ragged clothes on his back and a toilet kit," Deanna recalled. He was penniless. He admitted to her that he had "lived on the streets," that he survived by drifting through "restaurant jobs for a meal and a few dollars." Prior to his Vermont return, he had been working in New York City at a seedy hotel for the down and out.

Even as Dave decided to return to Vermont, he still struggled to face his family. Arriving in Waterbury, a destination for both buses and trains from the New York City area, he retreated to a motel on the outskirts of town. One day, as Emma Morse pulled into her driveway she spied a coat on the front porch. She at once recognized it as Dave's raincoat and surmised he was signaling that he was nearby. By then she had abandoned hope that she would ever see him again. Her life had been marred by loss—of an infant child, and of her husband Rex decades before. At one time she had told Helen Bell that she just could not hold out hope for Dave's return any longer.

Photograph by Aaron French

Dave with Aunt Emma Morse, circa 1994.

She found him at the motel, paid his bill and brought him home. He lived there with her before eventually finding housing in Morrisville, near Deanna. On the day Emma drove him to his sister's home, all Deanna's children came to the house to see Uncle Dave. In a horrible coincidence, as they sat in the kitchen, Dave's father, Hugh Morse, pulled into the driveway with his wife, the woman with whom Dave had caught him cheating as a child.

"I never heard Dave use the word 'hate'," Deanna said, "but that was as close as Dave ever came to that feeling." One of Deanna's children quickly opened the refrigerator door, pretending to clean it, thus shielding Hugh from seeing Dave at the kitchen table. The unexpected visit lasted only a few moments.

After a couple of days, Dave horrified Deanna by telling her he needed to return to New York, "to say goodbye to Sal." Sal and Dave had become friends. Sal operated the carousel in Central Park. As she put Dave on the train back to New York, Deanna thought to herself that she was seeing him for the last time. But Dave did indeed return, just a few days later, and stayed.

Dave lived at Deanna's house while he worked to re-establish a measure of financial security. He did not have a driver's license, a necessity to hold a job in rural Vermont. In order to have his license restored, he needed to pay off parking and speeding fines from decades before. "That was Dave. He would just park where he wanted," Deanna recalled. She remembers a Department of Motor Vehicles employee commenting that she had never known such old fines to be repaid.

Years before, Dave had asked Deanna to hold a US Savings Bond for him. It had been a gift from his mother about fifty years before. The accumulated value was $104.00. Deanna's husband, Ernest, told Dave to keep the bond. "I'll give you $104.00." It was a beginning. Dave then worked a series of jobs — furniture store salesperson, gas station-minimart attendant, clothing store clerk — to gradually restore his financial footing.

Deanna does not remember Dave speaking of a plan to re-enter the world of sports journalism. He seemed content enough with an entry level job and achieving a measure of self-sufficiency once again. Then, one day, Ken Burnham went shopping.

Burnham grew up in Hardwick. He had been a three-sport star

athlete at Hardwick Academy, the precursor to Hazen Union School. He was doing some part-time sports reporting for the *Gazette*, but was contemplating a move west. A 1965 graduate from high school, he was old enough to remember Dave's sports coverage for both the *Times-Argus* and the *Rutland Herald*. He dropped into Caplan's Store in Morrisville, an outlet for rugged, sensible clothing and footwear. At the checkout counter, he recognized Dave, who was tending the register. They struck up a conversation that quickly turned to Vermont sports history, a subject area in which Dave's knowledge was unmatched. Aware that the *Gazette* needed a full time sports reporter, Ken suggested to Dave that he give Ross Connelly a call.

In each of our lives there are moments, encounters, and relationships that forever change the arc of our stories. But for this teacher, this blind date, this sudden change in plans, this narrow escape from disaster, our lives would have turned out differently, or not at all. Certainly Dave's early life changed as key mentors stepped in, and so he found his way to a career documenting the athletic feats of young Vermonters. However, had Burnham not shopped at Caplan's and recognized Dave, the book on that pursuit in Dave's life would have closed in the fall of 1974, after barely a decade. He had made a mark, certainly, but he might largely have been a forgotten figure, now that twenty years had elapsed since his last Vermont byline.

Instead, he was about to reimagine himself in that role, and go on for twenty more years. The stories he would write in those decades would matter, but the events would have happened all the same. Burnham, or someone else, could have reported them. But the world did change for the athletes, their families, their coaches. An unforeseen love affair burst open in a corner of the Northeast Kingdom. Dave's passion and caring, not always expressed in eloquent syntax, but always intended to honor the athletes, shone through. He was everywhere one man could possibly be, talking with the coaches, the athletes, the townspeople who shared his memories of historical events. He would attend practices; he patrolled Main Street, waving, fist-bumping. As

I reflect on his life: his overcoming a challenging childhood, his early professional success, and his ensuing personal misfortune, his decades at the *Gazette* feel as close to a resurrection as a man can achieve without dying.

Near the end of his tenure with the *Gazette*, thinking back on his passion for sportswriting, Dave reflected on a quote by Vin Scully, the Brooklyn and Los Angeles Dodger broadcaster for sixty-seven years: "I've loved it since day 1." Dave wrote, "Maybe there's a lesson for me there. Can't do anything else."

As Dave settled back into the life of a Vermont sportswriter, he seemed not to skip a beat. Surely he too "loved it since day 1." His first column in the *Gazette*, February 2, 1994, reads as if he had been writing about local Vermont sports for thirty years without pause, not for only ten years, followed by a twenty year hiatus. Readers were treated to their first glimpse of his remarkable grasp of names and places across the spectrum of Vermont sports history. He describes driving to the Hardwick Elementary School, "past the Dump Donlin recreation field." Donlin had been a Little League coach in the 1960s. He had also brought Legion teams to compete in Barre when Dave was writing for the Times-Argus. He was a memorable character, to be sure, but he was one of hundreds of coaches whose stories Dave had told, one whom he had probably not written about in twenty-five years.

As Dave recounts his initial tour of Hardwick with Burnham, he continues:

> 'Right over there,' I recalled quickly, 'on the top row of the bleachers is where we would set up for your games.' That is when Hardwick Academy and Burnham, along with Jim McWilliams and others, were holding sway in The Green Mountain League and radio station WDEV of Waterbury was covering as many as seventy basketball games a season throughout the state.

Dave devotes most of that first column to acknowledging the work that Burnham had pursued in order to provide "singular, award-winning coverage the past four years":

> Burnham recognizes the vast void of local coverage, except for the continuing efforts of WDEV and Ken Squier over the years, and stretched the Gazette's reach past Hardwick and Hazen Union School to Craftsbury, Twinfield, Cabot and beyond. For his efforts he has been recognized as Vermont's weekly sportswriter of the year by the Vermont Press Association.

Dave sounds as if he has been immersed in the daily Vermont sports scene forever, not as someone who has been absent for twenty years. He concludes the column with a pledge:

> As the state basketball tournament will be upon us soon, that will be our immediate thrust, along with continuing coverage with the ski scene, especially Craftsbury Center. We also hope to offer coverage to snowmobile clubs, bowling leagues, and elementary school leagues. At the same time there has to be those getting ready for spring, especially those in garages looking forward to a new season at Thunder Road.

> To all those in competition and fans alike, I look forward to making the rounds of the weekly sports scene and continuing the work Ken Burnham started here at the Gazette.

In the space of a few hundred words Dave has revealed his

Vermont roots, his scope of knowledge, and the philosophy of his coverage — not just the higher profile secondary school and national-level athletes, but the elementary schools, the snowmobilers, and the bowlers as well. Lastly, he also demonstrated the humility that would mark his tenure through the coming twenty years.

During his years writing for the *Gazette*, Dave's recall of athletic events, achievements and milestones across the Vermont sports world grew to legendary status. As he settled into his new office space in 1994, he could remember back thirty years to when he covered a group of local boys, many of whom still lived in Hardwick— Brown, Putvain, Mercier, Strong, Burnham, Colbeth, Renaud, Brochu. Across the 1963-64 academic year they had reached the state semifinals in soccer, the finals in basketball, and lifted the championship trophy in baseball.

The 1964 Hardwick Academy Terriers' run to the state baseball title included wins over Bristol, Proctor, and Enosburg. Of those three games, the semifinal battle with Proctor was best remembered, a twelve inning pitching duel between Jon Dimick of Hardwick and Ray Pentkowski of Proctor. Hardwick prevailed 2-1. Both pitchers went the distance; both allowed eight hits, both struck out fourteen. The winning run was driven in by Ken Burnham. Jon Dimick pitched all three playoff games for Hardwick, allowing just one run over 30 innings while striking out 41.

Jon Dimick's story is another piece of Hardwick athletic lore with which Dave was very familiar from his years at the *Times-Argus*. Recall that he had been present when a pro scout offered Jon a minor league deal. A lefthander with a dominant fastball and nasty curve, Dimick had excelled across high school and Legion competition. High school and American Legion teammate Dave Brown recalled Dimick's mastery, "Everything was down and hard." Dave had covered the clashes between Dimick and Brown's Barre Legion team and Carlton Fisk's Bellows Falls squad. A perfect example of Dave's presence across the world of Vermont sports, and of his memory of events across decades, centers on one of the pitching match-ups between Dimick and Fisk. The game was at Bellows Falls' Hadley Field where Fisk had already achieved legendary status for having struck a mammoth home run far beyond the left field fence. On this day, Dimick struck out Fisk in his first three at-bats, but Fisk doubled his last time up, driving in the winning runs.

Years later, Dave partook in a Hardwick Village Restaurant gabfest that featured the collective recollections of bygone moments of athletic prowess. When the topic of Fisk's blast off of Dimick came up, the storyteller was heard to say " … but then Pudge finally caught up with one of Jon's fastballs and …" Softly, Dave interjected, "I think it was a curveball, down, at the ankles." Of course, they checked it out; of course, Dave was right.

In a July 1994 column, Dave reached a bit further back in local sports lore to write of a Birdie Tebbets-led barnstorming collection of Red Sox matching up against a team from Hardwick in October 1949. Jon Dimick's father, Wendell, who played minor league ball, struck out both Johnny Pesky and Dom Dimaggio.

Across the road from the Dimick home, Wendell built the finest local ballfield. A natural amphitheater, it provided fans with perfect viewing along grassy banks above the playing surface. Michael Clark fondly recalled piling into cars — without seatbelts — for the winding three-mile drive from town, tracking the course of the Lamoille River, to watch or play games there. Just beyond the outfield, a bend in the river dictated the curve of the fence and limited the expanse of the field, such that "official" Legion and high school games could not be played there. Still, Clark describes it as the most beautifully manicured surface, painstakingly maintained by the Dimick family, a labor of love.

Dave's sterling recall allowed him to connect events he covered in the present to those he had witnessed decades before. Just as the Hazen Union Wildcats basketball success echoed the Spaulding team Dave covered in the early 1960s, so too did a 2006 pitching duel parallel the state semifinal Dimick-Pentkowski match-up that Dave would have remembered from '64.

The dominant pitcher for Hazen in 2006 was Tristan Southworth. Hazen reached the state finals for the first time in twenty-five years. Through the four tournament games, he pitched so many innings that Dave referred to the new rule, put in place for subsequent high school seasons to limit a hurler's workload, as 'the Southworth rule.' After closing out the semifinal game in relief, Tristan authored another overpowering performance, going the distance in the final, marred only by back-to-back doubles in the eighth inning, leading to 1-0 defeat.

Chapter 10

HARDWICK GAZETTE
A Resurrection, 1994-2015

That Dave's return to the world of Vermont sports journalism took place in Hardwick has an "of all places" feel to it. From his upbringing in Waterbury, and along his career path through Barre, Springfield and Rutland, Dave had lived and worked in towns that served as regional employment and population hubs. In the 1990s, Hardwick's population hovered between only 2,500 and 3,000.

Hardwick is just thirty-five miles from Waterbury, yet its more troubled economic history can make it feel a hundred miles away. Even the 2014 Hardwick Town Plan uses the phrase "down on its luck community" to describe the era between "granite capital" and "rebuilding center." The road from Waterbury to Hardwick passes through economically healthier towns: first Stowe, a thriving ski and tourism center; then Morrisville, home to Copley Hospital and several manufacturers, including Concept II, Turtle Fur, and HearthStone, the Vermont stove company. Copley Hospital serves towns within a twenty to twenty-five mile radius, including Hardwick, fifteen miles east along the Lamoille River.

Hardwick had a hospital once, but it was closed by a state commission in the 1970s. That decision was vigorously opposed by many townspeople, as it felt like one more affront to a town struggling through a dearth of good fortune.

*   *   *

In the early twentieth century, Hardwick had been much stronger economically. An 1868 town vote in support of the Lamoille Valley Railroad ultimately put Hardwick in position to serve as a hub for the granite industry some decades later. Woodbury, the township immediately to the south, boasted a number of granite quarries. In 1897, the Woodbury Granite Company built a rail line spanning the six miles between the quarries and Hardwick village. Over the next twenty years or so, granite sheds prospered as sites for cutting and polishing the stone that was then shipped across the northeastern and Midwest United States. As many as 1,200 people were employed in the industry. Woodbury granite was a stone used for building, as opposed to Barre granite, known for its use in monuments. Although not the source of the stone, Hardwick named itself "The Building Granite Center of the World." A 1907 *Burlington Free Press* article described the Hardwick granite-processing operation as "the largest and most modernly equipped of its kind."

Granite from the Hardwick sheds was used in the construction of the Pennsylvania, Kentucky, Iowa, and Wisconsin state capitols. The Western Union Building in New York City and Union Station in Washington D.C. both stand on stone from Woodbury, via Hardwick. However, late in the 19th century, reinforced concrete, more easily available, came into wider use in the construction of foundations. Labor and freight costs rose, opening the way for less expensive building options to gain traction. The market for building granite dissipated. The last building of renown to include granite from Hardwick was the Western Union/AT&T headquarters on lower Broadway in Manhattan's Financial District, construction of which was completed in 1916. The last operating granite shed closed in 1934 following a labor strike. From then on, Hardwick was home to small mills and family farms, but had no large employer.

Still, the central village did not lack for commerce. Merchants consistently occupied the storefronts along Main Street. Lorraine Hussey, born in 1927, recalls that there was no need to leave town to shop. Two pharmacies, a grocer, a 5&10, two barber shops, a restaurant, a department store, a movie theater, a diner, a couple of bars/poolrooms, and the office of the *Gazette* filled both sides of the street. There were two large inns, one at each bend of Route 15 as it follows the course of the Lamoille River through town. Mrs. Hussey recalls no shortage of guests or activities at the inns. She and classmates enjoyed hanging out in the "dining room" of the Eagle Hotel as the restaurant was operated by the family of one of her friends. She fondly spoke of the numerous French (immigrants from nearby Quebec, Canada) family farms along Center Road, which traces a route across a series of hills and vales as it climbs to Greensboro, seven miles north. Several of those families had ten or more children. After matriculating from their local schools, many would attend Hardwick Academy, up on Cannon Hill, across from the Eagle Inn. There were few cars, as gas was rationed through World War II, so even local travel was limited.

As Dave and his sisters were growing up in Waterbury, Hardwick had developed a reputation as a tough, edgier town. During his tenure there, Deanna liked to remind Dave that she remembered being told when young that, "Nice girls don't go to Hardwick." Of course, as Dave quickly found out, and spent twenty years reporting, Hardwick was filled with as many loving and supportive households as anywhere he had been.

At a time that coincided with the downturn in demand for area granite, perhaps arising out of the Prohibition years, Hardwick acquired the nickname "little Chicago." There was extensive rum-running along the Vermont-Canada border through prohibition, but no more so around Hardwick, almost forty miles from the international border, than elsewhere. Mrs. Hussey, who went on to own a clothing store along Main Street for thirty years, thinks back on the war years and mid-century Hardwick as quiet, and even "boring," but not as troubled or violent.

Michael Clark, class of 1972 at the newly built Hazen Union School, remembers Hardwick having a reputation as a rough town, but believes that he and his friends paid it little mind. "We were aware our reputation wasn't so good, but we didn't carry it around; we didn't live it." His recollection is that growing up in Hardwick was "awesome." The next generation of children from the Center Road farms were his friends and teammates. They passed summer days at the local ballfield, a short walk from his house. His Little League coach was Dump Donlin, whom Dave remembered in April 1994 as he drove into Hardwick for the first time in thirty years.

Clark loved the main street, where "you could have them mix up a vanilla soda for you, or you could buy your fourth grade girlfriend a ring for five cents and it was a big deal." He fondly recalled the barber finishing up his haircut by asking, "Wanna little stinkum with that?" and slapping some cologne along his neck before he could answer. Both Clark and Mrs. Hussey remembered the Idle Hours Theater being packed on weekends, providing townsfolk with access to current Hollywood fare. Before it finally closed, in the early 1980s, it had begun to run X-rated films, which may have reaffirmed Hardwick's tarnished reputation for some.

In the early 1970s, Hardwick experienced some acts of vandalism, broken storefront windows and such. WCAX television, the CBS Burlington, Vermont affiliate, covered the situation, resulting in a degree of notoriety. Around the same time, the local police force experienced some attrition and encountered difficulty finding replacement personnel. In Clark's recollection, "We became (known as) the lawless town of Hardwick." In anticipation of a recurrence of trouble around an approaching Halloween night, an amped-up law enforcement presence was arranged. "And then Halloween was kind of a fizzle, but it was an eerie night," recalled Clark.

Outside of Hardwick, atop a hill at the end of several miles of dirt road, sits Coles Pond, a small body of water whose shore is dotted with a mix of year-round homes and seasonal camps. Residents of the area take pride in the pond, elevation almost 2,200 feet, as being one of the first locales to welcome winter and often the last to see ice depart. For some years, in the 1970s and '80s, Coles Pond was home to a "casino" of the same name. (It was actually a dance hall; no gambling took place.) Liquor was BYOB. It featured a floating floor that rocked as up to 200 people danced. Events there may also have linked Hardwick with an image of raucous behavior and brawling. Saturday evenings catered to "the moms and dads," in Clark's description. The featured music might have been a square dance band or an ensemble playing big-band fare.

Friday nights were a different story — the bands often came from as far away as Boston, played rock and roll, and drew younger crowds from a distance. The drinking age had been lowered to 18, so the crowds were large. Remembered Clark:

> "The place was getting packed. They were coming from St. J [St. Johnsbury], Barre and Newport [larger towns within a thirty mile radius], and you just knew there was going to be a fight, and it was going to be Barre-St. J, or Barre-Hardwick. Most of us were not fighters, so we stayed away, but every once in a while, 'Hey, we think it's starting out there, guys' and we'd go outside and there'd be a crowd of 150 people, and there'd be two, or three, or four guys in that circle, and just blood. It would be awful. I'd get sick to my stomach. That was a wild and crazy place."

Late in the 20th century, a subtle evolution began in and around Hardwick. There was no signature event to cite as a marker of change; it was more a coincidence of small business entrepreneurs basing their start-ups in the area. Dave Morse's Hardwick years coincided with that resurgence of economic vitality, centered mostly around value-added agriculture and the farm-to-table movement. Independent, innovative agricultural businesses led the way.

In 1996, Tom Stearns opened High Mowing Organic Seeds, a company that prospered as it positioned itself as small, hands-on and organic in a climate of growing suspicion around petrochemical fertilizer and mass

Times Argus file photo

Dave at the Hardwick Village Restaurant.

production of food. Jasper Hill Farm, a world champion cheesemaker, opened in 2003, a few miles away in Greensboro, a community within the Hazen Union School domain. In 2004, the Center For an Agricultural Economy was founded in Hardwick, designed to "support food access, farm viability and working landscapes." Hill Farmstead, a world champion brewer, opened in 2010, just up the road from Jasper Hill. A bookstore, two restaurants, a hair salon and a delicatessen joined the local food co-op on Main Street. That food co-op, founded in half a store on a tiny side street, expanded into a new space, anchoring the main street. The old Hardwick Inn, the architectural heart of the village, but mostly empty for years, benefited from an extensive rehabilitation, and leased out office space, including a fitness center and a clothing store. Ben Hewitt told the story of Hardwick's resurgence in his 2010 book, *The Town That Food Saved: How One Community Found Vitality in Local Food* (Rodale Books).

As Dave reacquainted himself with the village of Hardwick, he sought out company, conversation, good food, and history. The Village Restaurant was a good place to find all four.

Tammy Wetherell was young and new to waitressing at the time. She remembers that Dave took a liking to her, perhaps sensing her inexperience. They developed a repartee in which she would encourage him to eat healthily, and he would joke or deflect in reply. Dave always went to a corner booth so he could watch the front door and hail arriving patrons, alert to the possibility of a new reminiscence or sport-related legend.

Typical of relationships he forged over two decades in Hardwick, Dave's friendship with Tammy lasted until his death, across her comings and goings as a waitress there. Years later, his sports coverage included stories about her son Ricky's Golden Glove exploits.

As triumphant as Dave's return to sports journalism would prove to be, the beginning was troubled. Dave's instinct to retreat, to isolate himself when feeling unable to cope, remained. Early on, Connelly approached Dave about entering and filing his pieces on a computer, as he had been handing in typed, or even handwritten copy. The technology overwhelmed him. Behaving as he had when confronted with challenges at other times in his life, Dave fled. "He just flipped out and disappeared, went back to New York," recalls Connelly. It remains unclear just where he was. With Deanna's help, Connelly tracked down Dave's New York City friend, Sal, but he had not seen Dave.

On another occasion, when he and Connelly had a disagreement, Dave holed up in his Morrisville apartment, and refused to answer the door. Days passed, and he returned to the office. Deanna recalled yet another upset, triggered by a conflict at work, when Dave packed his car with a plan to move to Florida. Indeed, he drove all the way to his brother Don's home in that state. Again, the emotional storm cleared and he returned.

In a hopeful sense, one might explain Dave's overcoming adversity and returning to his post at the *Gazette* as evidence that he recognized he had found his way to a nurturing community, one that might help him heal old wounds. It is difficult to imagine a community more enamored of a sportswriter, but, sadly, his instinct to isolate himself during a crisis never completely left him. Such a pattern, as much as it might reflect an active choice, suggests to me that Dave struggled with a deep-rooted emotional pain that he was powerless to overcome on his own.

Connelly's tolerance for Dave's sudden absence undoubtedly reflected his need for a sports editor. He said:

> "Finding people with the skills to work at the Gazette was always hard. With Dave's background, I was eager to have him replace Ken, and think I was a bit in awe considering his experience. His skills were attributes I didn't want to lose."

In response to Dave's initial flight from the *Gazette,* Connelly reached out to Deanna, messaging through her to Dave that:

> "Writing on the computer would not be necessary. I emphasized I valued his work and what he was bringing to the Gazette, and didn't want him to quit."

These events took place soon after Dave's return to Vermont. Memories of New York must have still been fresh in his mind. Deanna suspected that Dave had retreated there. Wherever Dave did go, he returned to his Morrisville apartment not long thereafter. Connelly went to visit him and "reassured him repeatedly that he didn't have to use the computer, and that he was needed." To his great relief, Dave returned to the *Gazette*. Shortly after returning, he approached Connelly to ask if he could learn how to use the computer. He proved a quick study and entered his copy into the computer thereafter.

Regarding his ongoing relationship with Dave, Connelly said:

> "I knew he needed a job, loved sportswriting, and the loss would be the Gazette's if he stayed away. I also realized one had to ask Dave and never impose. That was how I interacted with him for the many years he was at the Gazette. The newspaper and I were better for it."

Tommy Gardner, *Gazette* reporter, reflected on sharing workspace with Dave.

> "He was always kind with me, but he occasionally had sharp words with Ross [Connelly] or Vanessa [Fournier, Gazette photographer]. Such disagreements were usually brief, and Dave would always apologize afterwards.

He could be moody or withdrawn at times. During these periods, Dave would engage less in office conversation. Such spells seemed unrelated to work; they were just a part of Dave."

Gardner's conversations with Dave at times touched on Dave's past, but rarely in detail. He recalls a "wistfulness" he detected in Dave. In describing his talks with Dave, Gardner employed a metaphor of a forest, in which one has a sense of areas of light or heavy undergrowth, and how that sense guides the conversation away from the darker locales.

Chapter 11

"THE MORSE CODE"
Dave's Column

"Yes, stories do get embellished with time. Otherwise
the facts are the facts."

— Dave Morse, 9/24/08

Ross Connelly did not ask Dave to submit a resume when he
applied for the position of Sports Editor at the *Gazette*. He
quickly realized that Dave knew exactly what he was doing.

> "It was such a pleasure having him there. Susan [Ross'
> wife - together they ran the paper] loved working
> with him. Every Tuesday night he would give her
> the layout, and it would fit perfectly, just from his
> experience."

He describes their work together at the newspaper as:

> "Not a traditional editor/reporter relationship.
> Whatever he wanted to do, he had the green light.
> I just let him write. And, of course, his Morse Code
> was the best thing."

In addition to covering numerous events each week, across a range of activities, schools and ages, Dave wrote a column he titled "The Morse Code." The column provided him an opportunity to exercise his voice across the world of athletic competition, to honor people from the present and the past, to provide lessons in Vermont sports history, to call out officialdom for losing sight of its mission: to facilitate athletic opportunity for youth. Dave often left the realm of sport, to write about jazz, a hide-away diner, even how to avoid the interstate while driving from Thetford to Hardwick:

> Coming back up Route 113 you go to Post Mills, Vershire to 110 in Chelsea, then 14. I followed the Northfield bus until it cut off for Williamstown, over the hill (partly dirt, bypassing Foxville).

And he used the column to celebrate friendship or to share glimpses into his past. "The Morse Code" might focus on one event, person or issue, or Dave would pepper it with remarks across a dozen different topics. Collected together, the writing covered a remarkable range of information and ideas. Dave's career at the *Gazette* fell just shy of twenty-one years, and in a typical year the paper published fifty-one editions. Altogether, he wrote over one thousand columns of "The Morse Code."

In the column following the death of Henry Jurras, his *Times-Argus* mentor, Dave wrote:

> Jurras presented me with an "AP stylebook"— the Bible, as it was, to a copywriter from WDEV, jingles and such stuff.

Yet Dave's style was far from an eloquent prose. He could switch tenses, ignore conventions of punctuation, follow a train of thought all his own. The above quote leaves it to the reader to sort out that the copywriter had previously only written "jingles and stuff," whereas it might be taken that the AP stylebook was a 'how to' on jingle composition. He wrote at times colloquially; at times in snippets; at times in run-on sentences. Malapropisms occasionally appeared that might further puzzle his reader: "auspices" became "auspicious;" "perfunctory" became "prefunctionary;" "conscience" became "conscious."

Dave Frederickson, a high school basketball coach in both Arlington and Bennington, won over 500 games and founded the Vermont Basketball Coaches' Association. He laughed as he recalled Dave redefining a word when prodding him for awards information in advance of a banquet, promising, "You can tell me. I'll keep it embargoed." Thus, a reader unfamiliar with Dave, or his subject matter, might become frustrated, particularly if a sequence of events, such as the flow of a game, was being discussed. Yet, the positive tone, his respect for the athletes, and his passion for the games invariably prevailed.

Dave often found occasion to speak fondly of his own mentors, including Henry Jurras, high school principal Dac Rowe, and Clyde Hess of Camp Abnaki. As Dave embraced the opportunity to step outside the traditional definition of sportswriter and re-imagine himself as a mentor, he allowed his readers insights into the people and places that helped shape and guide him. As reluctant as he appeared to shed light on his life during the twenty years leading up to his arrival in Hardwick, Dave took a very different approach to his early years. He recognized that, despite early hardship, he had experienced success. Good fortune had led him into the spheres of influence of wise men who opened his eyes to a path in life, who provided him with a moral code, and who molded him into a sportswriter. He did not forget.

In September 1994 he wrote of Dac Rowe, then 97 years old and living in nearby Peacham, "a noted Vermont educator, still playing cards and splitting wood." When Rowe died just fifteen months later,

Dave began his tribute with a brief life history and then,

There's so much more. Oh, so much more. Mr. Rowe brought out the best in everyone, especially his students, regardless of who you were.

After trying out for the cross country team, taking a wrong turn, and getting lost, Mr. Rowe made me his manager. I was allowed to make out schedules, call in results, resulting in a sportswriting career.

Photograph by: Brendan Buckley
Dave with young fans at the Baseball Hall of Fame in Cooperstown, New York.

It wasn't just me, he took everyone under his wing. He once told a runner who finished last in a race he should take up music. It became a career.

There's no getting around it, Mr. Rowe was stern!

Girls were called 'Miss', boys by their last names. 'Yes sir. No sir.' He only had his students' best in mind.

Further on in the remembrance Dave recalled his high school senior class trip to New York to see the Dodgers at Ebbets Field, and the Yankees' opening day game vs. the Red Sox in the Bronx. Not surprisingly, the group from Waterbury, Vermont, were Red Sox fans. Of a key development in the game Dave wrote:

> Ike Delock raised Mr. Rowe's ire to the extent he wanted to go on the field and wring the neck of the Boston pitcher, and probably had a clear path if we didn't intercede. Delock threw a 3-1 fastball to Mickey Mantle that the Yankee slugger deposited off the facade. Mr. Rowe's resulting tirade was true passion.

And finally, and prophetically, given the relationships with many "young people" he himself would develop, Dave closes the column:

> I write these notes for the young people who may read them. I would hope every student and athlete could have the kind of relationship we all had with Mr. Rowe. Everyone is a winner.

> One last note. Mr. Rowe also had a sometimes unknown passion for poetry. He wrote "Play the Game," which was read at his service. That is what is left for us to do.

Henry Jurras lived to age ninety-eight. He had been sports editor of the Barre-Montpelier paper for more than forty years. Dave described him as "kind and gentle," even though he was running a department on deadline:

> It took Henry three months to ask LeCours if he would mind covering the desk so he could have a day off from 4AM starts [an afternoon's deadline was 11AM at the time] and he was the BOSS!

How telling that Dave refers to his principal as 'Mr. Rowe' and his newspaper boss as 'Henry'! He hardly needed to use the words 'strict' and 'gentle' to differentiate these men. His terms of address are enough information for us to imagine those relationships.

*   *   *

Camp Abnaki celebrated its one hundredth anniversary in 2001. Dave wrote about the camp then, and again in 2011, when his younger brother Dexter joined him in a return to Abnaki. On a summer weekend, they toured the eighty-nine acre property set on Grand Isle in Lake Champlain, and drove to the top of Vermont, Mount Mansfield, where they had first hiked as campers, and later, when they grew into counseling roles, led groups of campers. Of the Camp, Dave wrote in 2001,

> I wrote for the Abnaki Herald back then, which has been published since "Dad" Clark founded camp in 1901, the second oldest in the country. Ken Kern chronicled our conquest of Mount Mansfield way back then, sleeping outdoors at the top of Vermont……
>
> Bang the drums slowly, but let the roar of the campfire, its spirit, and meaning live on!

Dave was enamored of sports and games from an early age. He found his way to a life spent reporting about games, and yet, in this passage, he places his love of Camp Abnaki above those games. Upon his death, his ashes were spread at the Camp.

When Dave and brother Dexter visited Abnaki together in 2011:

> Dexter and I were drawn back in time. We knew we were close when we reached the sand bar. The motto

remains, "Help the other fellow." Close your eyes, and the sounds will be the same as when you were here. Now open them: Kids' faces are the same too, in pure wonderment. Kids frolicking at the second oldest boys' camp in the country....more than 150 campers, and not a computer in sight.

Then, recalling excursions to Mount Mansfield, Vermont's highest peak:

At Camp Abnaki in the '50's it often fell upon myself to herd groups....I couldn't resist telling the story of stopping in at the old Summit House with campers, and being refused service in the main lodge, no doubt because of our condition from days and nights on the [Long] Trail. The Summit House isn't there any more. Its last day was May 31, 1956, my hiking heyday I guess you could say.

Dave Morse; thanks to Vermont Mountaineers

Henry Jurass / Robin Roberts reunion, 7/21/2003.

From 1935 to 1952, minor league baseball thrived in New England. Jurass loved the game and followed it closely for his paper. The Northern League player best known for having started his career path with the Twin City (Barre and Montpelier) Trojans was Hall of Fame pitcher Robin Roberts. During Roberts' time in Vermont, the 1946 and 1947 seasons, he and Jurras became friends. Dave was on hand to document the renewal of that friendship more than a half century later, when Roberts returned to help celebrate organized baseball's renaissance in Central Vermont.

As early as 2001, Dave hinted in his column that Vermont might field a franchise in the New England Collegiate Baseball League, a summer wooden bat league founded in 1993 for college players. He was on the mark: in 2003, the Montpelier-based Vermont Mountaineers played their inaugural season.

The Roberts-Jurras reunion took place that first season, on the occasion of Robin Roberts Night. At Montpelier's Recreation Field, a relic of Depression-era government-funded projects, Roberts climbed up into the stands to greet his longtime friend, then 95 years old. Dave's photo of the handshake appeared alongside his Gazette column that week.

> Hall of Fame, class of '76, as an original Philadelphia Whiz Kid, Roberts requested Jurras be present at Recreation Field.....Frail and unsure of his footing at 95, Henry stayed seated in the grandstands of his youth. Roberts, now 78, rushed from the mound of his lasting fame up a few rows with a big hug and a whisper. It no doubt had to do about playing pool away from the field of battle.

In his homage to Jurras, Dave included this Roberts quote, "I don't think we were as good as he said, but he was. He made us look a lot better than we really were." Until his death in 2010, the Hall of Famer made a number of trips back to Montpelier for Mountaineer events.

When the Mountaineers offered Dave work as their publicist for the 2003 season, he embraced the opportunity to champion his favorite sport, and took a leave of absence from the *Gazette*. In that role he worked closely with the team's general manager, Brian Gallagher.

Gallagher marveled at Dave's work ethic, his knowledge of baseball and of Vermont's baseball history, and at the connections he forged with the team's personnel. Jurras' and Morse's professional alma mater, the *Barre-Montpelier Times Argus*, sponsored the Mountaineers. Gallagher expressed amazement at how regularly Dave would scoop the *Times Argus* on Mountaineer news. Occasionally Gallagher would feed the *Times Argus* a scoop because he felt guilty at how consistently Dave beat them to the punch. "Dave did the hard work," he recalled, "He called me twelve months of the year for news of prospects, alumni and schedules. He was never satisfied with just a box score and game summary. It was not unusual to see him at our away games around New England."

Gallagher laughed as he recalled accompanying Dave to his car one day, as Dave had saved copies of the Gazette to give to the General Manager. The car was scattered with old newspapers and magazines, but somehow Dave knew just where to find what he was looking for. He seemed not even to notice the mess; the car was his second office.

An organized baseball presence in Vermont was important to Dave. Vermont's short spring season, invariably characterized by gray skies and a range of precipitation from rain to snow, challenges high schools and colleges across the state to complete their schedules. Smaller schools sometimes struggle to fill out their rosters; in such instances students are permitted to play for a different school than the one they attend. Through the early 2000s Dave wrote of high schools dropping baseball due to diminishing interest. He decried the University of Vermont's decision to drop the sport in 2009. In March of 2010 he wrote:

> UVM will not have an opening day for baseball in well over a century ... What's going on here? Beats me, with all the UVM riches from postseason NCAA basketball and hockey appearances they can't play baseball in the backyard.

He strove to keep his readers attuned to the sport: I counted mention of the Mountaineers in over 130 of Dave's columns from

2003 through 2014.

At their annual Hot Stove League Banquet during the winter of 2014, and again with an on-field ceremony that summer, the Mountaineers celebrated Dave for "writing stories about the Mountaineers that provoked great interest."

An especially engaging feature of Dave's writing was his long view of Vermont sports history. His memories and his own experiences spanned decades. In writing about one person or event, Dave's narrative would typically spill over to a related tale. He found ways to make connections across sports, regions of the state, amateur and professional play, and generations. His coverage of one person in particular illustrates that approach.

Charlie Smith was born in Craftsbury in 1918. At five feet, seven inches and 130 pounds, he was not an imposing figure, even by pre-WWII standards. But as a high school athlete he was dominant across a range of sports. He led Craftsbury, classified then as a "junior" school by student population, to a dramatic upset of the state "senior" basketball champion school, 30-25, scoring 21 points. The game report described him as a "brilliant forward," (at five-foot, seven!). "Imagine that a mighty mite would topple them in their lair."

Also, during those Vermont winters, Smith was a dominant skier, winning the "interscholastic down mountain skiing." He went on to the University of Vermont where he became the starting catcher on the baseball team. While there, one of the pitchers on the staff was Mickey Cochran, who went on to create a ski run on the slope behind his Richmond, Vermont home. He raised a family of US Olympic downhill ski racers, Marilyn, Barbara Ann, Bob and Lindy.

Charlie Smith later served in World War II, fighting across Europe in the Battle of the Bulge. One day, his cavalry unit played a baseball game against a battalion featuring a Hardwick Academy alumnus. St. Louis Cardinal star Stan Musial was also on that team. In 1949, Charlie played with Wendell Dimick, whose son Jon would one day be a pro prospect pitching for Hardwick Academy, against a barnstorming team of major leaguers managed by Burlington, Vermont native Birdie Tebbetts, who himself enjoyed long career in the major leagues as both a player and a manager. After the war, Charlie became a basketball official, rose through the ranks, and one day refereed the New England high school championship game at Boston Garden — Winooski, Vermont vs. Charlestown, New Hampshire, a team that starred Carlton Fisk at power forward.

In the years that Dave covered Hardwick area sports, Charlie Smith was a regular attendee at soccer, basketball and baseball games. Unsurprisingly, his grandsons were three-sport athletes. Across twenty-one years, Dave wrote of these links in several columns, mining the same material, but tacking from a different approach each time. In doing so, he connected dots from Crafsbury, Vermont to Boston Garden, from the 1930s to the 2000s, from basketball to skiing to baseball, from high school to college to professional level play. Wherever the storyline led, a reader could trace its path through Vermont sports history along Dave's beat.

Dave's memory bank was responsible for many of the threads he followed across people and events, but he also employed his reporter's

Photograph by Patty Coultas

Dave observing a Hazen basketball practice.

skill. Away from athletic venues, he was a familiar sight in town, walking the length of Main Street, from Connie's Kitchen at the junction of Route 15 and North Main, up the hill to the Hardwick Village Restaurant, with the *Gazette* offices conveniently in between. He would spend hours at a booth or table, holding court across conversations with any townspeople who might stop in. His phone linked him to every other source of Vermont sports information. Dave brought the same curiosity for detail that Brian Gallagher admired to all his work.

As Dave settled into his new job in a new town in the mid-1990s, a love affair developed between him and his readers. It was nurtured in several ways. Above all was Dave's work ethic - across at least eight towns, spread over several hundred square miles, Dave covered scholastic competitions from elementary through high school. He unfailingly cast the student-athletes in a favorable light; he found reason to write about the last child on the bench as well as the stars. If there was a day without a game to cover, Dave would observe a practice. He visited with the athletes to learn their stories. Ryan Renaud, Hazen Union class of 2001, remembered that Dave's presence at a practice prompted everyone to hustle just a little bit more. A story he told reflected Dave's approach. Renaud started on the 2000 Hazen championship basketball team. He recalled that his greatest basketball asset was that he stood six feet tall. In his humble recounting, the team's scoring and athletic ability were weighted to the other four starters.

> "This is where Dave comes in. Obviously he couldn't write about my offensive exploits, so in one article he called me a defensive specialist - not a bad bone in the guy's body, had to write something positive about everyone. I remember reading it, getting a laugh out of it and that was that. The problem was: Coach Hill read it too, and Dave's writing in the Gazette was gospel, so now Aaron is thinking I really am this 'defensive specialist'. For the rest of that year, and my senior year, Coach had me, potentially the slowest guy on the court, guarding the best player on every opposing team!"

Surely Renaud is underselling his ability and contribution — the team did win the state championship, but his story underscores Dave's intent to emphasize the positive in each student-athlete.

Dave's affability was unmatched. He would chat with anyone close by. And, it can't have hurt that his appearance stood out: a shock of thick white hair, parted and combed, balancing out a matching magnificent white walrus mustache. At a game, walking down Main Street, or behind the wheel of his car, he was impossible to miss. His visibility was enhanced, some years into his tenure at the Gazette, when the state champion Hazen Union basketball team included him in the group to receive a championship jacket. Dave wore his red, white and blue parka with pride. When a fellow sports journalist challenged his ability to remain impartial, Dave replied, "I've got nothing left to prove." Taking note of Dave's decision to wear his Hazen jacket, one obituary writer said, "Nor did the fairness of his coverage change."

Hazen Union basketball, the highest profile program on Dave's beat, won the state title five times over his twenty years. His reflections upon those triumphs cemented his connection to the players and staff, first in 1996, barely two years into his tenure. From his column:

> Deja vu! As in all over again, the same way. It was fifteen years in the making, but Hazen Union and rival Peoples Academy of Morrisville were back on the dance floor at the palace of Vermont basketball. The Wildcats waltzed off with the 1995-96 Division III crown at the Aud Saturday, just as Hazen had done against its rivals in 1981.....

> The basketball coaching staff at Hazen likes to say the Wildcats were 21-0 in claiming the boys' first state Division III in fifteen years...

> The coaches take responsibility for the three losses....It's the style of head man Steve Pratt, in only his second stint of a promising career. The first to point to six strong returning seniors, Pratt and the Wildcats rallied around last year's near miss of going

to the final four at the Barre Auditorium...It motivated
them all season.

Everything to gain and nothing to lose. As they
say— the rest is history, and it's on Hazen's side.
Deja vu.

Four years later, Pratt's assistant coach, now his successor, Aaron
Hill, coached Hazen to the first of his state titles. Again, a core group
of seniors were the heart of the program, and this group had grown
up with Dave. He knew them well and wrote:

This is truly a storied group at Hazen Union, with
two players and a coach having started at the varsity
level as freshmen, and being joined by six others
along the way to a common goal. It hasn't always
been easy.....nothing is that is truly worth it. Randy
Lumsden and Billy Welcome are the players and
Adam Gann the coach; he was sent to the sidelines
as a sophomore with a heart ailment. No less a
person could handle what Gann has had to endure.

For the most part, the trio has been in the middle of an overall four
year record of 66-24, including three straight final four appearances
at the Aud in Barre, highlighted by Hazen's first state title since 1996.

The third Hazen title that Dave covered was won in 2006. That
team featured only three seniors, two who had been classmates for
twelve years, and a third, Brad Mader, who joined the team in his
sophomore year. At six feet, eight inches tall, he provided a low-post
presence that anchored a stifling defense, and forced opponents into
double-teaming him, freeing up outside shots. Dave's story touched
on the senior leadership and the developing tradition of a parade of
cars escorting the team bus as it returned home, along Route 14, to a

celebration at the House of Pizza, owned by the parents of one of the players. He wrote,

It never gets old and brings tolerable meaning to

photograph by Patti Coultas

Dave at the Aud with Tanner Benjamin following Hazen Union championship, 2009.

mud season. Only the cast changes, right down to the raucous trip 25 miles over and back on Route 14 to the Barre Aud. Wherever there were pull-offs, the faithful reassembled to get behind the Wildcat Special (Tom Dunn at the wheel) and the caravan, which was accorded an HPD escort from the Burnham Hill water tub.

And:

'We are a team,' stated tri-captain Troy Lemay, suiting up for the final time since third grade with cohort

Jamon Smith, and Mader, who came on board after his freshman season, as the lone seniors. Mader showed his Wildcat stripes by making everyone better around him.

Twelve years into his *Gazette* career, Dave's love for, and knowledge of, the Hardwick community is evident as he concludes his 2006 title coverage with a series of paragraphs devoted to the families of the players—Brad Mader's grandparents; Jamon Smith's athletic heritage in his mother, Patti, (nee Ainsworth) who led her Hazen teams to the Aud, and of course, grandfather Charlie. And he writes of the Lemay family philosophy — "keep it fun" — and of how or where other relatives, unable to be at the game, followed the action.

The last two Hazen champions that Dave covered were back to back titles in 2009 and 2010. The first of those teams included seven seniors, with two juniors making significant contributions. Both final four games were close contests, with Hazen's suffocating brand of defense proving the difference. Following the '09 championship Dave wrote:

It was the BFA Bullets waiting in line to take a shot at our Wildcats...The Wildcats responded as they had down the stretch to turn aside Thetford Academy in their semi....

Hazen had been jilted at the quarter-final altar on its own court of dreams after the latest title in 2006......

The train of vehicles back to Hardwick picked up steam by a greeting in Woodbury - a police escort in front and back of Tommy Dunn's Wildcat special. Flashing lights at 20mph for five miles. The largest gathering ever at the corner of Main and Wolcott...

Young female fans called WDEV on their blackberries, or whatever, to alert everyone of the estimated time of arrival.

'The party's on in Hardwick', declared (WDEV) host Leigh Kittell. [sic]

'We're going to open the House of Pizza', declared Nick and Artemis Vasiliadis; everyone just turning around at the largess of this wonderful family.

A year later, Hazen cruised through the final four with surprising ease against two rivals with whom they had dueled closely over the decade. But on this championship weekend they outscored their opponents 126-79. Dave chose to focus on a player who had not received much attention through the season.

Coach Aaron Hill wasn't quite sure if it was a hunch, but senior understudy Brandon McLeon had earned his keep to stay on the court in Hazen Union's stirring triumph over Lake Region Union Saturday at the Barre AUD.

'We talked about that,' said Hill of his veteran staff - family and friends - that make for the most successful program in the state, as the Wildcats were on their way to back to back championships, four in eleven seasons and five since 1996.

So, steely guard Adam Whitney came back on among four starters and McLeon remained the fifth in the final push.

photograph by M. Lange

Dave with Hardwick friends at Norwich University on the occasion of "Dave Morse Day"

'Oh my goodness', Hill would say, sounding the good fortunes of Wildcat nation, 'It was the game of his life. ....He was disruptive, difficult to play against.' And, something Hill values greatly, 'He's a senior. He earned it to stay out there.'

Six more seniors graduated that spring, thirteen in total from the repeat champions. That proved too much for the returning underclassmen to overcome. A three-peat was not to be. 2010 was the last championship Dave covered.

Dave found joy in writing about schoolchildren. As much as he marveled at their athletic feats, he was drawn more to their spirit, their dedication, their teamwork. His conversations with them were not limited to their sports participation. As Billy Welcome, Hazen class of 2000, said, "He asked me about home; he asked me about school, what I wanted to do."

The Wildcat Pride

Volume 1   Edition 11   2005 - 2006   Hazen Union

2005 - 2006 Hazen Union Yearbook Dedicated to Dave Morse!

Hazen Union, Hardwick, VT

We dedicate the 2005 - 2006 Hazen Union Yearbook to Mr. Dave Morse, long time sports writer for the Hardwick Gazette.

For many years he has supported the student athletes in this school and written wonderful write-ups about them in the local newspaper. Over the last four years,

he has supported the seniors in every sport they chose to pursue and helped them find colleges suitable to their needs and wants. Everything Dave has to say should always be taken seriously because it's good advice. Anytime you see him, on the court or in the hall, stop and say "Hi." Maybe he has a connection at one of the colleges you're interested in.

Photograph by Al Foss

Hazen Union 2006 yearbook dedication.

Dave received numerous honors in recognition for his work. Of course, he deflected that attention as best he could. He never suggested that he was undeserving, but his message in light of those awards was unchanging, stated in different ways but always boiling down to, "It's my privilege to do this work, and my work is all about the athletes."

Long before he arrived at the *Gazette*, Dave had been singled out for his work. In 1968, less than three years into his tenure at the *Rutland Herald* he was named Vermont Sportswriter of the Year by both the Vermont Press Association and by the National Sportscasters and Sportswriters Association, most likely in recognition of his coverage of that year's Winter Olympics from Grenoble.

In 1999, just five years into his return to Vermont sportswriting, he was once again honored by the Vermont Press Association as Sportswriter of the Year. The following year, 2000, the Vermont Basketball Coaches' Association honored Dave with their Media Award. Other awards and recognition followed: during the summer of 2002, on the occasion of Norwich University Media day, the school elected to label it "Dave Morse Day." The following edition of "The Morse Code" included these reflections, in which Dave cast light upon his prior mentors, and his own good fortune:

> Ken Wild, our managing editor at the Herald, passed on his passion to all of us. I was able to work at the Herald because of earlier guidance from my Uncle Rex, Dac Rowe, Clyde Hess, Rusty Parker, Ken Squier, Brian Harwood, Henry Jurras, Harold

Reynolds and many others.

It wasn't about me....but the incredible cross section of folks who were under the tent on Sabine Field are what makes Vermont such a special place, and well wishers who have called, written, or stopped me on the street.

I want to make it abundantly clear it has been the community of Hardwick and surrounding towns and their young people that have given this humble guy a new lease on life in these last 8 ½ years.

In 2003, the Vermont Principals' Association included Dave in the inaugural Hall of Fame media class.

In April of 2006, Dave was inducted into the New England Newspaper and Press Association Hall of Fame. Later that same year, the Hazen Union graduating class dedicated their yearbook to Dave. It was one of the two honors across his life that touched him most deeply. He later told others that it, and the February 2014 commemoration at Hazen Union, meant more to him than any other recognition or award he had received. He included this message to the class of 2006 on the *Gazette* sports page that week:

The significance of your honor of dedicating this year's Hazen Union School yearbook to me is that it comes as a complete surprise, which I will cherish above all other good fortune forever.

This comes from the people I admire and cherish the most.

Your graduation coincides with my 50th high school

reunion to the day. Both reasons to celebrate.

Always be kind of heart. Happiness, success and
long life to each and everyone. I look forward to
talking with each of you many more times.

Over twenty years, across the many school communities he covered,
inevitably, tragedy intervened to take a young life. Dave included in
his column his memories of, and his tributes to, the deceased. Dave's
own grief emerged in his writing, echoing that of his readers. He also
wrote of those who had lived well into old age. He wrote of friends
and colleagues best known to him, and of townspeople whose deaths
were mourned by an entire community.

Typically Dave's remembrances were a catalog of commentaries
from those in attendance at a service or memorial gathering, but he
would include his own thoughts as well. A tribute to one who lived a
long life can be a celebration of that life; a tribute to the young reflects
the tragedy of that loss. Several times Dave documented the end of
too short a life.

Of MacKenzie Pratt, a star athlete at nearby Lamoille Union High
school, Dave wrote,

We have lost another great, twenty-one year old
student athlete. The effervescent MacKenzie Pratt
succumbed to cancer...'Why not me? I can handle
it' she was famous for saying....Handle it, and with
class...I remember a hug or two Mac was famous
for...this special and remarkable person always gave
her best, and brought it out in all others she came in
contact with.

And following the death of a basketball player, Krystian Paduzzi,
from nearby Twinfield Union High School, he wrote:

It was hard to go to the gym on Friday evening...For the second time recently tragedy struck the Twinfield Union boys' basketball team. Krystian Peduzzi, a junior, died the previous afternoon in an automobile accident....Krystian contributed in so many ways. Why so young? None of us have those answers. It strikes home. How precious things are, like going to the gym.

Dave Morse; courtesy of the Morse family.

Tristan Southworth.

And, when cancer took another young life:

Everything we take for granted each day in life was tempered last week by the loss of young Luc Gates of Enosburg High School. The three-sport star succumbed to the hemorrhaging of a brain tumor at age eighteen.

A very likable young man, Luc could always be found exchanging greetings with opposing players, and with fans, before games....

> Luc led a near complete comeback against then-
> undefeated Hazen in the recently completed
> basketball campaign.
>
> Luc reminded me of the buoyancy and brilliance of
> the late Harmon Bove....Like Harmie, Luc motivated
> others to do their best at all times, as he did. Their
> lives were all too short - for which we don't have the
> answer - but each left a legacy that will carry on.

The above reference to Harmon Bove reflects Dave's high esteem for those who elected to join the military. In addition to the respect he had for his uncle Rex Morse, and for his high school principal Dac Rowe, both veterans of world wars, Dave had known two soldiers who died in Vietnam. One, Louie Washington, was a young man whom Dave had counseled at Camp Abnaki. The other was Harmon Bove, a star athlete from Burlington who had been drafted by the Houston Astros in 1968. After one minor league season he enlisted in the Marines and died in 1969, just shy of his twentieth birthday. His stepfather was a sportswriter and Dave's friend. On two other occasions Dave would remind his readers of Bove's story while memorializing fallen soldiers.

Jesse Strong died in Iraq in 2005. He was from the hamlet of Albany, Vermont, and attended tiny United Christian Academy in Newport, on the Canadian border. Prior to one summer during high school, his life had not overlapped with the boys from nearby Hardwick and Cabot until he joined them to form a Babe Ruth League baseball team. Once that season was done, he again went his separate way. In those few weeks he made a lasting impression on his coach, Dan Hill, and his teammates. Dave wrote:

> They were just a bunch of teenage boys making
> their way and realizing they could play the game
> they loved. Their good nature and character were

captivating. Strong made an immediate and lasting impact....slender, but with the quickest bat. Strong had the brilliance of one Harmon Bove. This is a prayer of thanksgiving for the Strong family for sharing such a gifted son with all of us.

In August of 2010, Tristan Southworth, a 2007 graduate of Hazen Union, was killed in a firefight in Afghanistan as he tried to rescue a wounded comrade. Prior to joining the military, Tristan had been a high profile presence on the local sports scene for more than a decade. His home was in the hills of Walden, a small village east of Hardwick that, even in northern Vermont, is known for the intensity of its snow and cold. The town has an elementary and middle school, but children travel outside the community for their high school years.

Tristan's early athletic success was as a dominant Little League pitcher. Hardwick and Walden were part of the same "region" for post-season competition, so Tristan became friends with Hardwick boys during those summer all-star tournaments. When it came to choosing which high school to attend, he chose against the prevailing wisdom, by joining the teammates he knew at Hazen Union, over the more highly regarded St. Johnsbury Academy. It proved a memorable choice.

Tristan excelled in soccer and basketball as well. He played for coach Aaron Hill for three years of the school's ongoing dominant basketball run. The teams were state champions once and runners-up once in that time. In baseball, as described earlier, he memorably led Hazen to the state finals.

Beyond his athleticism, Tristan possessed qualities that impressed coaches and peers alike. He competed at full intensity, leading by example with an effort that others were inspired to match, whether or not they brought the same level of athletic ability to the event. He had no swagger in his performance; his demeanor was focused; his attention complete. He looked out for every teammate. Following a game, even one that had been fraught with a male adolescent edge, Tristan's comportment through the post-game handshake line was engaging and respectful, using a first name when he knew the opposing player.

Tristan's mother, Julie, noted that Tristan developed a social awareness at an early age. She remembered him befriending a boy of color after he had been racially targeted. He wrote an editorial to call out bullying. He and Dave had forged a connection early on. While Tristan was still in middle school, Dave gave him a book about Jackie Robinson. It made a lasting impression, so much so that Tristan chose to wear the number 42 on his baseball uniform. Ross Connelly recalls that Dave carried a concern about race relations, and maintained a focus on that issue at area schools. He knew those few students of color in Vermont faced prejudice, and no doubt recalled the local nastiness he was confronted by at the time of his marriage to Marietta. Dave wrote a brief story about Tristan's tribute to Robinson, quoting Tristan:

> "I liked his attitude in the face of adversity, and what he has meant to everyone, not just in baseball. He has always been my favorite."

That last sentiment is one I am certain he shared with Dave. The article ended,

> "Southworth prefers to play short - Robinson's prime position - but has always been a top flight pitcher on his teams since Little League. Southworth opened at short, batting fifth, at Lake Region on Monday, with a social consciousness [sic] which will always serve him well."

Dave was crushed by Tristan's death. His column that week was headlined,

I WANT TRISTAN BACK!

He opened and closed his column with that line. The rest was mostly quotes from Tristan's coaches and teammates focused on intangibles, his defense, his effort, his selflessness. Dave included one other reflection:

Tristan Southworth threw two pitches - back to back - that Northfield High hitters deposited into right center field...producing the only run in the state baseball championship of 2007. One can age on these prospects of sitting around the fire and having one of those pitches back...That's not the option anymore. I WANT TRISTAN BACK!!

The Hazen Union gymnasium overflowed with mourners as Tristan received military honors on a Sunday in late August, 2010. On the occasion of his "Appreciation night" in February 2014, Dave concluded his remarks of thanks with these words: "And please always remember the sacrifices, and say a prayer for Tristan. Thank you." In one last connection between the athlete and the journalist, the gym would next be filled to capacity in April 2015, when Dave was memorialized by the community.

As an orphan himself, Dave must have been especially sensitive to those who lost a mother. On a few occasions he wrote remembrances that acknowledged the importance of a mother's contribution to young lives. Connie Kapusta, whose eponymous "kitchen" Dave so regularly patronized, died in 2010. Dave wrote:

Connie Kapusta left an indelible mark on all of us who

knew her and well beyond before succumbing to a long and courageous battle with cancer...Her sons... realized their dreams because of her dedication and devotion to family...Connie was champion of all seasons for her family and community.

Patty Renaud catered to Dave at the Village Restaurant. Her sons, Jamon and Ryan, starred at Hazen and helped bring home two state championships. She died of cancer at age 47. Dave remembered:

The last time I saw Patty Renaud was a couple of months ago. I didn't want to intrude, but Steve Pratt and Adam Gann, her nephew, insisted. We called Leo, and he said come ahead. I'm so glad I did. Patty produced a bunch of pictures. It was the good times, and she was genuinely pleased with the visit. The sports mom for all seasons...Patty was the first person to officially welcome me to the Hardwick and Hazen Union School communities. She sat down with me at the Village Restaurant, wanting to know who the new sports reporter was at the Gazette...No one had ever done that for me before. I will always remember the gesture. That's how important all the youth of the community was to Patty.

In 2011, Ross Connelly's wife, and co-editor, Susan, died. Dave had worked closely with her. Their son Sawyer had grown up in the *Gazette* offices. That same week, Hurricane Irene tore north through central Massachusetts and ravaged Vermont, wiping out bridges and roads, stranding families. The hardest hit population center was Dave's hometown of Waterbury. Dave's column sounded a deeply mournful tone:

Hearts are heavy here at the Gazette. We have lost our beloved Susan...We took particular pleasure each week in the first sports page...Her involvement was complete, of course. Susan cherished Sawyer's soccer games....the Gazette is a virtual museum - a legacy she and her husband wish for Hardwick and the region....Susan didn't get to the Island and Wallace Pond...but she can look down upon them now.

It has been a long and trying week, otherwise, too. Waterbury is where I went to high school....Turn the corner on Randall Street and one wonders how waters reached from the Winooski [River] to the second floors and across to the new fire station on South Main Street. They were the homes of the Robies, St. Onge, Magnus, Burnham, Berry. Complete family possessions lining the street. The outpouring has been gracious and complete in the Vermont manner.....Heavy hearts aplenty.

The last remembrance Dave penned, only months before his own death, commemorated Diane Hill, wife of varsity baseball coach Dan, and mother to head basketball coach Aaron, and his assistant Travis, who had led Hazen Union to that first basketball championship in 1996. He wrote:

This is personal for me. The extended Hill families have been such staunch supporters of mine since arriving in Hardwick twenty years ago. Diane Hill's loss will be felt by everyone in her hometown and beyond.

I was so pleased my brother Dexter, who passed five months ago, got to meet everyone at an AAU basketball game. They had so much in common with their dignified fight against such odds.

My image will always be the Hill family at Hazen Union basketball games - coaches across the way, grandchildren playing in their little 'sandbox' - the bleachers. What better family settings. Everyone should try it.

They will be my combined strength for years to come.

Chapter 12

"BE PART OF THEIR LIVES"

D eanna once said to me, "David never cared about gaining wealth. He'd give away everything. If you needed a dollar and a quarter, and he had a dollar, he'd find you that quarter."

In Waterbury, Barre and Rutland, the three Vermont towns where Dave plied his trade, he participated in community events and activities on behalf of school aged athletes. He was a Little League coach in Waterbury, youth baseball administrator in Barre, organizer of statewide athletic events and banquets in Rutland, and mentor to student interns and young reporters. Only in Hardwick did he so passionately and charitably involve himself in the community at large, and with families in particular.

Was this degree of caring a conscious response to his recognition that he had been given another chance at the life he once embraced, but then had lost? Can we possibly fathom how he processed the course of his life, from foster child to successful journalist, to heartbreak, to homelessness and journalist again?

Many who knew him before he arrived in Hardwick remember him as a quiet, kind and conscientious classmate, colleague, counselor and mentor. Whatever the psychological forces at play, which we cannot fully understand, within a few years of arriving in Hardwick, Dave began to reach beyond the bounds of his profession to lend a helping hand to some of the athletes he covered. *Gazette* owner Ross

Photograph by Vanessa Fournier

Tim Shedd greets Dave at his appreciation night.

Connelly observed, "He had such a shitty childhood. He looked out for kids who needed help or guidance." In Dave's own words, the most he ever said on the subject was, "I'm just doing what others did for me."

One former colleague of Dave's marveled at how generous Dave was in helping others. He wondered how Dave could afford to be so generous on a reporter's salary. Deanna spoke of Dave's reluctance to spend money on himself. She believed that Dave's magnificent mustache, such a distinguishing feature of his appearance, was a ploy designed to hide his poor dentition. In the same way he deflected attention towards others, he directed his money elsewhere as well.

He did not make much money at the *Gazette*. He was paid for each article he wrote, and was reimbursed for his travel costs. He enjoyed the freedom that arrangement allowed him— no set schedule or required office hours.

The answer to the question, "How could Dave afford to do what he did for those kids?" is that his aunt Emma, who died in 1997, had left Dave a small inheritance: a fairly new car and some money. At the time of her death, Dave had told Michael and Helen Bell, to whom Emma had left her Waterbury home, that he planned to protect that money and use it to "do good."

Chapter 13

MEMORIES OF UNCLE DAVE
Paying It Forward

Tim Shedd, class of 2001, is, as of 2022, Hazen Union High School basketball's all-time scoring leader with 1,695 points. Even though he was one of the taller players, his forte was the three-point shot. He helped lead Hazen to the 2000 state title, and was named Vermont High School Player of the Year in 2001, an honor not typically awarded to a small school star. He went on from Hazen to play Division-III college basketball in New England. Of the hundreds of athletes Dave covered over two decades in Hardwick, he forged his closest relationship with Tim. Tim lives and works in North Carolina, so most of his conversations with Dave, after college, were by phone or Internet, but he believes they managed to touch base weekly through the years.

Tim credits much of his own personal success to Dave's reporting. Such was Dave's influence across the world of Vermont sports that, even after a twenty-year absence from that beat, his opinion mattered. Tim believes that Dave elevated his profile enough to garner the votes for Player of the Year, and also to draw attention from nearby Norwich University, where he played for four years, and earned an engineering degree, "at almost no cost." That education led to his career in North Carolina, where he also volunteers as a basketball coach in youth development leagues.

Tim had traveled back to Hardwick in 2014 to attend Dave's tribute event, and returned one year later to deliver one of the eulogies at his memorial service:

> "I'm 33 years old, and this is one of the greatest honors thus far in my life…I was granted the ability to pay tribute to an incredible man, and for that I am truly grateful…If success in life is measured by your ability to enrich the lives of others, then Dave Morse was one of life's greatest champions… He was a master craftsman; this community was his masterpiece…If you missed all your shots in a game, but made one, Dave only focused on that one shot…I am going to miss his voice saying, 'Oh, my

gosh, it's Timmy Shedd!'

I am going to miss reading his column, and feeling like I was still connected to the community.

Lastly, I am going to miss his voice saying, 'I love you, big guy.' These are the last words I heard from Dave, and I will hold those words in my heart forever."

Tim was one of three Hazen athletes, during the summer of 1999, whom Dave drove to Five-Star Basketball Camp in Pennsylvania. None of the boys' parents were able to leave work to transport them there. In Tim's words, "Dave was the first guy to raise his hand, and he helped pay, too." Today, those three young men look back upon that occasion as a zany road trip with "Uncle Dave." (They initially christened him Grandpa Dave, but he objected). Tim recalls a night in an off-the-beaten-track "Addams Family" motel that was freezing cold, as was the breakfast it served the next morning, "like out of an ice chest." "Dave said, 'We gotta get out of here,' and we made tracks."

In a theme that would be repeated in summers to come, Dave introduced himself to the camp director and coaches, and made sure that they were aware of the gifted Vermont players attending the camp. It mattered not that the camp was known as the "mecca of summer basketball," and included NBA superstars among its alumni. Tim recalls with amazement the day he saw Dave engage in conversation with Howard Garfinkel, founder of Five-Star.

Billy Welcome was another of the Hazen three to attend Five-Star that summer. Looking back on that trip, he said, "Five-Star would not have happened for us without Dave. He helped us fund-raise, he chipped in himself, he drove us there, he paid for lodging and meals, and then he stayed all week talking us up: 'Those three young men are named Randy Lumsden, Tim Shedd, and Billy Welcome and they attend Hazen Union High School in Hardwick , Vermont.' The camp was filled with dozens of D-I basketball coaches, and players, but (to Dave), Randy, Timmy, and I were the main attraction."

The following summer, Dave extended his reach to nearby Stowe, including their star player, Dana Martin, in the group he brought south that year, to two camps, Eastern Invitational in New Jersey, and Five-Star in Pennsylvania. Martin went on to star at Skidmore College and then play for a local minor league franchise, the Vermont Frost Heaves.

In his reflections, Tim Shedd recognizes that, absent Dave's reporting, the Hazen basketball program would still have thrived, and won championships, but he strongly believes that Dave's coverage fueled the community support that embraced the team, and certainly spurred its enthusiasm. "Dave saw the community as his family, and he cared deeply."

In recognition of Tim's special connection to Dave, at the memorial service Tim was presented with the Hazen state championship jacket that the team had given to Dave in thanks for his support.

*   *   *

Mike Baker, a 1992 graduate and basketball alumnus of nearby Peoples Academy in Morrisville, has taught at Hardwick Elementary School since the late 1990s. He joined Aaron Hill's coaching staff, and has overseen a hugely successful JV program at Hazen through much of Aaron's tenure. As his children, Isaiah and Jaden, grew up, they knew Dave and, as was typical, when an opportunity arose for Dave to arrange something special, he did. Such an event was at a Mountaineer home game that Mike attended with his sons, and with his nephew, whose father was serving in Afghanistan. Dave visited with them during the game and then arranged for all the boys to meet, and take photos with the players following the game.

Mike also shared this memory when his son Isaiah pitched for the local Little League All-Star team, and the opposing team hit Isaiah pretty hard and won going away. Following the game, the boys were distraught, Isaiah in tears. Dave came over to console them, and then offered to treat them all to a creemee — Vermont's name for soft-serve ice cream. Spirits were assuaged, and smiles returned.

Isaiah and Jaden, Hazen classes of 2021 and 2023, respectively, featured prominently on Hazen's basketball teams. During a conversation that highlighted his many memories of the special kindnesses that Dave performed on behalf of local athletes, and of the excitement and pride for school and town that his coverage engendered, Baker wistfully acknowledged his regret that Dave had not been there to cover his sons' stories. It was something he had allowed himself to imagine before Dave's death.

*   *   *

Brendan Greene grew up a few miles south of Hardwick in Woodbury, a hilly, wooded community lined with dirt roads and dotted with dozens of small lakes. Beyond sixth grade, most children from Woodbury attend Hazen Union. Brendan loved basketball, but he arrived in middle school feeling like an outsider. His parents had moved to Vermont from "away," so neither had a history or family in Vermont, and Brendan began seventh grade not knowing many of his classmates. But Brendan could play basketball. He was quick, with excellent court vision, and Hardwick basketball fans took note. Brendan believes that Dave sensed Brendan's initial feeling of "not quite belonging." Dave took the time to talk with Brendan, learn about him, and praise his play. Remembers Brendan, "Half the battle is believing in yourself. Dave made sure that you did." They would talk about Vermont sports history and famous athletes, and Dave would check in as to how Brendan was doing. "It was never about himself, always about you or the team."

When Brendan reached high school and began playing for the Hazen varsity, he became interested in attending the summer camps that other Hazen boys had benefited from. The camps were expensive. The community often held fund drives to assist local athletes. Dave sponsored multiple athletes, and he often provided the transportation to and from the camps, held usually in Pennsylvania or the New York metropolitan area. Brendan attended a camp at Fordham University. Most of the other attendees were local players. Brendan recalled:

> "Kids from New York who could really play. And I remember how Dave seemed to know all the coaches, and he told them about me, as if I was a top 100 prospect! That was Dave."

Years later, while in college, Brendan would call Dave from time to time, to check in, to tap for advice and encouragement. "He always made me feel important."

It wasn't just the kids that Dave would look out for; he provided a supportive word for coaches as well.

Alan Delaricheliere coached the Hazen baseball team in the years after Tristan Southworth and teammates reached the state finals. Interest in baseball seemed to have waned, such that Delaricheliere was left without enough players to form a team one spring. Dave approached him to chat one day. The coach recalled:

> "I told Dave that I felt like a failure. For the first time, this school couldn't field a team. Dave told me, 'You keep working; they'll come back.' The next year we had enough for a team. First practice, Dave stops by, 'See, Coach, I told you.' He made a believer out of everybody."

Steve Pratt coached the Hazen Union basketball team in the early 1990s and helped build the foundation for the school's emerging dynasty. In 1996, he led the Wildcats to their first championship in twenty five years. He had previously coached the varsity boys' basketball teams at two other area high schools, and remembers that Dave "put the best possible spin on it" when the first of those schools chose not to renew his contract. By the time Pratt arrived at Hazen, Dave knew him pretty well. Recalled Pratt:

> "He believed in what I did for the kids. Dave Morse forever impacted how I feel about myself. He loved others; he was a loving friend."

Billy Waller, a star three-sport athlete from nearby Cabot, went on to coach basketball at his alma mater. One winter night, they were scheduled to play at Craftsbury. A storm made travel hazardous, so Waller tried to have the game postponed, to no avail. When the Cabot team arrived at the gym, only three snowmobiles were parked outside. Remembers Waller:

> "The gym was empty of fans, no parents. No one wanted to be there. I didn't want to be there! Only one ref made it. I remember asking Dave, 'Dave what are you doing here? No one cares.' Dave's article about the game described the roar of the crowd encouraging the players on!"

Travis Hill, Coach Aaron Hill's younger brother, had starred on the first Hazen state basketball championship during Dave's tenure at the *Gazette*. He reflected upon the magic of Dave's coverage and his mission to promote local athletes. He credits Dave with creating the Hazen basketball phenomenon:

> "He wrote so many wonderful articles about the kids, people wanted to come and see what he was writing about. He restored pride in the Hazen community. He loved to introduce us to people:

one time he introduced me to a Division I baseball coach, someone who might be coaching future major leaguers: 'This is Travis Hill. He played on Hazen Union's 1996 championship basketball team.' He made it seem as if that coach should feel lucky to meet ME! I had the best sportswriter in the world covering my games."

Ricky Welcome echoed that amazement at how important Dave would make one feel. Ricky was another Hazen basketball player who benefited from Dave's help with fundraising for summer basketball camp and then drove with Dave to Pennsylvania. For Ricky, two moments from that trip stood out.

"First, the night we stopped at a motel, Dave got a phone call. Turned out it was his sister calling to wish him a Happy Birthday. He was turning 65 and spending his birthday making sure I made it to basketball camp!

The next morning, Dave gets up early and heads over to the camp. When I arrived there later, people were coming up to me. 'You're the Welcome kid from Hazen, right?' There were future D-I and even NBA players there, and Dave had built me up like they should be privileged to know me! This is before they had seen me play; by the end of the week they weren't so excited!"

One last thought from Ricky Welcome recalls Dave's own childhood, and the importance of caring people in the lives of children:

"Billy and I lost our father at an early age. This community raised us. At the heart of this community are the Hazen Wildcats, and Dave Morse is the godfather of the Wildcats."

Ricky's older brother, Billy, echoed these sentiments:

> "Over twenty years in Hardwick, Dave was instrumental in creating a sense of family. He had a profound impact on my life, starting when I was thirteen years old. He taught me how to treat people, care for others, and become a better man."

Randy Lumsden was another key player for the 2000 championship team, alongside Billy Welcome and Tim Shedd. He and his siblings were raised primarily by their mother. Dave recognized Randy's athletic ability when he was participating at the middle school level, and perhaps also saw some of himself in the young boy coming of age amidst challenging circumstances. Randy recalled Dave approaching him following a sixth grade tournament:

> "Dave came up to me afterwards and told me he was looking forward to seeing me at Hazen in the upcoming years. That was a big deal at that age, that little bit of acknowledgement.
>
> When I was a little kid I always wanted to get the Gazette, read my name in there. Dave gave me the encouragement that made me want to be a good athlete, to do good things."

His relationship with Dave continued through high school and beyond. Dave occasionally took Randy to breakfast at the Village Restaurant, during which he would share stories of covering Carlton Fisk, or memories of past games.

In contrast to all the memories of Dave's acts of kindness and affable disposition, one event stands in stark contrast. Scott Calderwood, father to Zander, another of Randy's teammates, described the scene that unfolded at an away playoff baseball game against Poultney High School:

> "Randy was on the mound for us, and the Poultney crowd, right up against the backstop, were letting him have it. They were jeering and on his case big time. The umpires didn't say anything; no Poultney school official stepped forward to stop it. Between innings, Dave left the stands and walked onto the field to confront them, and he blistered them for their unsportsmanlike behavior. He was furious. I'd never seen Dave so upset."

I reminded Randy of that occasion and asked about his own recollection of the scene:

> "I was a little shaken. These fans were hanging off the backstop, directly behind home plate. They were heckling me pretty good. I remember Dave going over. You know he had that shaky voice. He was pointing his finger at them. I couldn't really hear what he was saying, but he was giving them the business. I wish I could have heard what he was saying."

Poultney won the game 6-5, scoring in the home half of the seventh (final) inning. Dave's story bears no mention of the heckling. Reflected Randy, "That's the way we are in Hardwick. We don't make excuses."

Upon the occasion of Randy's graduation from Hazen, Dave presented him with a card. Randy said:

"He wrote me a really nice card. I wish I still had it. I can't remember the exact words, but he praised me, told me how proud he was of the person I was becoming, the steps I was taking in my life. He actually gave me $200. He didn't have a lot of money. I didn't have a lot of money either. I think he knew that, so that's why he did it."

Randy attended nearby Johnson State College. Dave came to all his home basketball games; he kept in touch. At Hazen games they would visit and catch up. As Dave was dying, Randy recalled:

"Aaron, Travis and I went down to see him during his end-of-life care, said our goodbyes, hugged him."

That was fifteen years after Randy had graduated from Hazen Union.

In the early 2000s, Brad Mader moved to Greensboro, Vermont to live with his grandparents. He entered Hazen Union as a second semester freshman. To that point, he had been raised in the northwest. He had a close relationship with his grandparents, as he had visited them over several summers. Brad's reflections eloquently capture the power and importance of Dave's presence in the lives of young athletes. Some of his thoughts echo the experiences of others, but they also contain very moving individual reflections. From an email Brad wrote to me:

"It is a tough endeavor, as I am sure you are aware, to capture the story of a man who consistently made the story about everyone around him.

Dave was always there. Always. I don't mean that in any passive way. In truth, Dave's way of being present and supportive was possibly the most stark example of selflessness that I have had the privilege to experience.

When you had a bad game or were generally struggling, he was there with encouraging words to lift your spirits, and when the opposite was true he would celebrate your accomplishments. He was never the loudest voice in the stands, or someone who would rush you at the end of the game, but he was always quietly there, attentive and supporting.

He would always include the facts of the event, but never resorted to focusing on any individual failure. Even when things didn't go our way, he always focused on the positives: Outstanding performances by opposing teams and players, outstanding performances that just came up short, displays of sportsmanship, etc. This was true in person as well. It's not uncommon for a high school athlete to have a rough game or series of games, and Dave was always there to listen to you and reassure you that you would overcome.

I do not think there is a way for me to accurately state or even know the positive impact that knowing Dave has had on my life, but I know that it is significant. I truly could not have more respect or love for the man. He was a great and selfless friend, and he is dearly missed."

One last memory captures the importance of his presence. In 2005, Brad attended the same summer basketball camp as Brendan Greene.

He was playing poorly, somewhat overwhelmed by the physicality of the other players. During drills on the second day Brad was amazed to see Dave standing courtside "a ten hour drive from Hardwick." Although his play improved somewhat from that point, Brad still fell short of a strong performance. Nevertheless, he remembered:

> "I can say with certainty that Dave showing up that weekend, at a time when I felt lonely and discouraged, and offering a friendly face and words of encouragement was more impactful than he will ever know."

*   *   *

The athletes whose exploits Dave covered for the *Gazette* are now young adults, even approaching middle age. Many of them have maintained a connection to organized athletics through coaching. As evidenced here, through their recollections of his kindness and caring, Dave's influence remains powerful. I believe that they will carry forward his spirit as they work with youth in their communities, just as Dave carried forward his experiences from Rex Morse, Clyde Hess, and Henry Jurras.

Chapter 14

ILLNESS AND DEATH
2014-2015

In the last months of 2014, Dave fell ill. Tragically, typically, he shared the news with no one. He continued to fill the sports pages with game coverages across his wide beat. "The Morse Code" appeared each week through the end of the year, without a hint that anything was amiss.

Dave kept to his daily routine, appearing at the Village Restaurant every morning, but Lynn Delaricheliere, who was so accustomed to his unchanging patterns, began to notice a difference in Dave. Initially, his standard two pancake order dropped to one. Sometime later, he stopped asking for side orders. Eventually he eschewed orange juice, substituting in a glass of water. Lynn had come to know Dave quite well over the couple of years she had managed the restaurant. As busy and diligent a worker as there is in Vermont, Lynn works several jobs. Her pace of movement and conversation allow her no tolerance for evasiveness and misdirection. Having watched his appetite gradually wane, she had asked Dave if he was having stomach trouble. He brushed it off as a minor issue that would soon resolve.

However, when Dave's appearance and dress began to suffer, Lynn probed more directly, and told me:

> "He started coming in disheveled, with the same shirt
> he had on the day before; his pants were dirty. One

day he came in with two different shoes. I started getting a little nosy, and he actually was not offended. He got it. He said, 'I've been to the doctor's, Lynn.' I said, straight up, 'Do you have cancer, Dave? He replied, 'I'm not sure I have cancer. I'm just having a little trouble with my stomach.' I said, 'No, you're not. You're going down quickly. You need to get looked at.'

And again, there was that line - you couldn't cross it."

Courtesy of the Morse family

Dave and Don Morse, circa 1945.

That line. The line that Dave had drawn between himself and the world at other challenging moments in his life, a line that sealed in so much personal information and emotion that he felt unwilling or unable to share with others, even friends or family. It was a state of mind that left him isolated, whether as a young parentless boy, as a failed college student, as an abandoned husband, as a destitute man in New York City.

There came a point beyond which Dave could no longer manage alone, could no longer shield his friends and colleagues from what was happening. Lynn's impatience with his rapid decline, and his ongoing reassurances, trumped her tolerance of the information barrier that Dave had erected. One day he told her he wasn't attending that night's basketball game, and then two days came and went without his appearing at the restaurant. Lynn remembered:

> "There was a day he came in and just sat with a glass of water, writing. He talked of retiring. 'Maybe this is my time.' I knew he was in trouble - you don't come in here?! You come here every day at the same damn time! If you don't come, you tell us you're going here, or to a game. You don't show up for two days?! I go looking! I crossed that line the day I stood at his apartment door and yelled, 'You're going to open this fricking door, or I'm going to kick the damn thing down!' I was livid, I was so pissed I wouldn't stop, because I knew he was in there."

Photograph by Nancy Welcome

Hazen Union basketball alumni celebrating Dave.

Dave's January 21st, 2015 column was headlined, "Under the Weather, On Top of Things." His last stories appeared the following week. Unable to care for himself, Dave was briefly hospitalized, and then opted to live his remaining days at a nearby nursing home. He died on March 28th, 2015. He was 77 years old.

On Saturday, April 4th, more than 500 people attended his memorial service in the Hazen Union gymnasium. Later arriving attendees stood on tiptoe and craned their necks from doorways to see across the crowd. Parked cars lined the road outside the school entrance. The April 8th edition of the *Hardwick Gazette* published the reflections of nine people who had known Dave — athletes, coaches, journalists, friends. These spoke to his ability to inspire young athletes, to his concern for their well-being, to his behind-the-scenes efforts on the behalf of many, to the role he played in rallying the communities he covered, and in fostering enormous local pride, to his encyclopedic knowledge of Vermont sports, and to his remarkable mustache, "the best facial hair in Vermont."

Chapter 15

AND IN THE END
Two Photographs

At the appreciation night held in Dave's honor the year before he died, Aaron Hill's son, Carter, still in elementary school, stood nervously at the podium to deliver this hopeful wish to Dave, referring to his own teammates:

> "I really can't wait for you to write a 'Morse Code' about Isaiah [Mike Baker's son], or Xavier [Travis Hill's son\]."

Dave shouted out, "I will!" Carter continued:

> "I've always been wondering about the heartbeat of Hardwick…(gesturing towards Dave)..He's right there!"

Dave stood to reply, "The heartbeat of Hardwick is young kids like this!"

Eight years later, Carter and Xavier, and Isaiah's younger brother Jaden, led Hazen Union to another state basketball title. Sadly Dave was not there to document the occasion, but memories of him, sitting up in the corner press box, his "office," were in the minds of the Hazen faithful.

Perhaps because he lived much of his life alone, there are not many photos of Dave, especially from the decades before he arrived in Hardwick. His sister Deanna and her son Aaron managed to find a couple from family gatherings. His signature mustache did not appear until the 1980s. Initially it was gray, but by 1994, as he stepped into his role at the *Gazette*, it had blossomed to a magnificent polar bear white, helping create the image that most of those who knew him will conjure up forever in their memories.

From the limited collection of pictures that I gathered, two stand out. They serve as poignant bookends to Dave's life. I first saw the earliest of the two in a frame on the wall of Deanna's apartment. It filled one half, the left side, of the frame. In it, young Dave and brother Don, bundled in snowsuits on a clear winter day, grin happily for the camera. On the right side, Dexter and Deanna, similarly dressed and posed, share their joy at being outside, immune to the Vermont cold. The setting is the same for both pictures.

Clearly they were shot on the same occasion, around 1945 or 1946. Deanna remembered those photographs as having been taken during the brief time that the family of six were together, when their father worked as a farmhand in Duxbury, when their mother was still alive. The expressions of glee across the four young faces match one's expectations as to how children ages two through seven should appear, blissfully happy and innocent, without a care in the world. But the world soon changed for the Morse children. Their nuclear family dissolved, as Hugh lost his job, and as Corinne fell fatally ill. Thus, that photo glimpsed Dave during a rare moment when all was right in his childhood world.

The second photo was taken in late summer 2012 in Ogdensburg, New York, along the shore of the Saint Lawrence River, at the occasion of Billy Welcome's (Hazen Union class of 2000) wedding. It was taken at night, well on into the reception festivities. The light is low, the focus a bit shy of sharp. It features a group of young men, in dress shirts and slacks, forming a circle. Each has an arm raised overhead in a gesture of celebration or solidarity. At their center, directly facing the camera, his head at shoulder level of the others, stands Dave.

Hazen Union's class of 2000 arrived at the school in the fall of 1994, half a year after Dave had joined the *Gazette*. Until Billy Welcome and I had a conversation in 2021, Billy had long assumed that Dave "had been at the *Gazette* forever." The first class that Dave followed through its six years at Hazen held a special place in his heart. This is how Dave described the scene captured in the photo:

> "A reunion of one of Hazen Union's most glorious eras, primarily the 2000 group. This tale starts even five or six years before then. That's about my timeframe here too.....Mike Burnham and Zander Calderwood joined us for what I guess passes as a 'mash' on the shore of the river.
>
> 'We are Wildcats, mighty, mighty Wildcats! Once a Wildcat, always a Wildcat!'
>
> Someone took my camera. I indulged in dancing and high fives, only.
>
> By now the band was playing, six hours after the exchanging of vows; ocean-going barges passing in the night, up the Saint Lawrence River, the lights of Prescott, Ontario on the other side.....There's 17 to 18 years in 30 hours, and you're on your own again."

*   *   *

Dave had turned 75 in May of that year. For much of his life, love had proven an elusive presence. He had glimpsed it in childhood, and at occasional holidays with siblings, nieces, and nephews through adulthood. In midlife, his wife had abruptly abandoned him, and he had passed the ensuing two decades mostly alone. Surely, on that 2012 summer evening, he recognized that his life and work had made a difference in the lives of others, and he felt the love and caring, which he had demonstrated for others for so many years, returned.

Dave Morse's Speech at his Appreciation Night, February 2014

I actually know everyone here. It's the greatest feeling in my life. To come into this building and see Timmy Shedd, everyone else, to see Tristan Southworth's family.

I would be remiss in not crediting Vanessa for the photos she takes to make the copy look better.

I have mentioned to Aaron a couple of times, yes, it's been twenty years as of early this month. Aaron keeps track of those things. If I ever made a good decision in my life, it was coming to Hardwick. I mean that with all my heart. I was born in Morrisville. Do you believe THAT?!

My first newspaper job was the Times-Argus with the great Henry Jurras. I worked with Ken Squier. I covered those great Spaulding teams that you sometimes hear about, even if it's 1962, '63, '64, something like that. This outsurpasses anything, and I could get Frederickson to say that—he won five. We don't figure to ever lose. Yeah, you're gonna get beat a couple of times, but you're gonna come back the next day and win. And that's what these young people are all about.

[Dave pointing.]

You know, I just saw Ryan Hall. Coach Hill was asking me about great things that have happened. Remember his shot against Williamstown in the Tristan Southworth game? That's what this town is all about, people coming out, sharing.

For Brittany to do what she did. We all know—the quote from Travis is so important: everybody is in this together; always has been, always will be. Waller was the same way at Cabot—those guys tore the roof off the Auditorium. That has to be shown around town at special gatherings, because that's what this town is all about, always will be about.

I kept trying to make some notes, but I'm glad I didn't bring anything from home just because this is a singular moment to me.

[Gesturing to the audience.]

The present day Wildcats here, they're gonna keep coming! We saw one earlier tonight, [pointing to Carter's sister] Lettie too!

But, yeah, once a Wildcat, always a Wildcat. And, please, always remember the sacrifices, and say a prayer for Tristan. Thank you

Acknowledgments

As I embarked on this project I was one person set on honoring the life of a wonderful man. Very quickly I learned that I was anything but alone. Instead, I became the medium through which hundreds of memories of Dave Morse would pass onto the pages of this book.

The wish to tell Dave's story had been on my mind since his death in 2015. It was not until late in 2018 that I began the work. My first connection was with Dave's sister, Deanna. We knew each other a bit, as we had spoken by phone around the time of Dave's illness and death. I visited her in her apartment, excited to at last learn the story of Dave's life. I was surprised to learn that, first, Deanna and Dave had spent years of their childhoods apart, and, second, that Dave had dropped out of sight "for quite a while." What lay before me was a very different journey than the one I had anticipated. Two yawning time gaps, absent many witnesses, needing filling.

I traveled to Rutland, Vermont to search the archives of the *Rutland Herald.* There, a receptionist led me to Tom Haley. Having no idea who I was, Tom welcomed me, sat me down, and began to tell me stories. As he spoke, he would occasionally interrupt himself to note, "Oh, and you have to talk to so-and-so; here's their number." And, of course, in the small world that is Vermont, degrees of separation are few–Tom's leads led to others, and so on.

Over the next three-plus years I tracked down and spoke with, or e-communicated with, dozens of people connected—many quite directly, a few only by quickly vanishing strands of association and coincidence—to the arc of Dave's life.

As much as this book is a biography, I know that it might also be termed an homage. I was intent on telling the story of a man I knew to be kind, generous, and honorable. Each time I dialed a new phone number, or clicked to send an email to a person I did not know, I worried about what I might discover. As I reach the end of this journey I am relieved and amazed to have heard Dave described in similar terms from those who knew him across the seven-plus decades of his life. In fact, some of those quoted here heard of this project and reached out to me, as they felt it important to share stories of his helpfulness, his warmth, his calm capability.

I contacted a number of organizations to aid in my research. Of those, I spent the most hours at the *Hardwick Gazette* and the Vermont State Archives. In times of COVID-19 precautions, on-site visits were carefully regulated, but Dawn Gustafson unfailingly welcomed me into the *Gazette* offices to search back issues, and the state Archives staff in Middlesex, Vermont were ever gracious and patient with my requests for old volumes from their vaults.

I first learned that Marietta was from Wyoming, Ohio when I reviewed her and Dave's wedding certificate. To learn that the town had a Historical Society was a pleasant surprise; to discover that it was staffed by Shirley Sheffield was a great gift. Shirley was "all in" on this project from the beginning. She not only did research on the Ohio end, she also provided me with an education of the tools available to me as I delved into Dave and Marietta's pasts.

Robin and Jill at the Sagadahoc Historical Society in Maine similarly seized the initiative to look in places I would not have thought of to help find traces of Marietta's years there.

Auburn Nelson, librarian at The Schomburg Center for Research in Black Culture, replied to my shot-in-the-dark email, and helped lead me to the *New York Times* notice of Marietta's 1962 nightclub gig in New York City.

Wiz Dow warmly welcomed me into the Hardwick Historical Society space in our old railroad depot. She found photographs and provided helpful suggestions as I worked to verify certain facts. She shared her University of Vermont Masters thesis about the Hardwick granite heyday, saying, "Use whatever you want."

Tom Haley and Deanna French each gave me a list of names from their respective circles to interview. Deanna and I spoke regularly about my progress, and about any new discoveries either of us had stumbled upon, up until her death in November 2021. Tom Haley kept abreast of my progress with periodic phone calls. Each of them helped instill in me the belief that this effort was a worthy one, and that I could see it through.

Among Dave's professional colleagues, Ross Connelly, the *Gazette* owner/publisher, and Mike Donahue, once Dave's intern at the *Herald*, and then reporter for the *Burlington Free Press*, were both prompt and willing correspondents to whom I reached out repeatedly. Ted Ryan, Dave's *Herald* colleague, welcomed me into his home based on one email introduction.

Among those I interviewed along the way, many fiercely believed in this project because they saw the importance in sharing Dave's story. "I owe this to Dave," was a regular refrain. They had known and loved him, been helped and supported by him, and movingly related their memories.

Included in this list are Dave's nephew, Aaron French; Hazen Union graduates Billy Welcome, Tim Shedd, Randy Lumsden, Brittany Lumsden, Ryan Renaud, Zander Calderwood, and Brendan Greene; Hazen Union basketball coach Aaron Hill; former US Ski Team member Peter Graves; and Hardwick Academy alumnus Dave Brown. Tristan Southworth's parents, Mike and Julie, sat on our deck one day to tell of Dave and Tristan's special bond.

I owe a debt of thanks to Mara Meehan, flower girl in her youth at Dave and Marietta's wedding, who welcomed a "blast from the past" when I blindly reached out to her forty-five years after the ceremony. Similarly, Marietta's stepdaughter, Carol Levesque, thirty years after Marietta's death, corresponded with me through Facebook to paint a portrait of the life and home Marietta helped create in Maine.

Many other people from across Dave's life are quoted here. Those quotes reflect hours of conversation, and a multiplicity of emails. I am grateful for the willing and cooperative spirit each of those individuals brought to bear. Again, I believe that spirit speaks to a collective belief in seeing Dave's story told.

Through the writing process I was shadowed by two readers, both gifted sportswriters. Alex Wolff and Len Shapiro responded without hesitation to read my manuscript, and provide edits, encouragement and advice. How very lucky I was to benefit from their insights.

I mostly retired from the practice of medicine as I began this project. It is difficult to keep such an effort a secret when one is doing little else. My family knew I itched to tell this story, and have followed along at every step. Our children, Matthew and Emma, are grown now, but they were Dave's subjects once; they knew him; they were buoyed by the stories he wrote; they remember his kindness. I have loved sharing my progress with them, and they have celebrated that progress with me.

My wife Helen was given little choice but to endure the day-to-day fits and starts of this work. As part of her misfortune, she was forced to sit through multiple oral renditions of my manuscript. She was, quite literally, my sounding board. Yet, she kept smiling and confirming her belief in my work. Her support never wavered. Through the disappointments and successes along the way, that support boosted my confidence and provided me with the energy to continue. This would have been so much more challenging without her.

About the Author

Brendan Buckley was born in 1951, three months after his Irish-born father and Australian-born mother arrived in New York City. He was raised in New York, but, from early childhood, spent summers in a small cabin at the foot of Mount Greylock, Massachusetts' highest peak. It was there that he fell in love with New England, and at Middlebury College where he narrowed that affection to Vermont.

After teaching sixth grade for two years, he pursued a career in medicine, and gained admission three years later. He did his internship and residency at the University of Massachusetts Medical Center and then moved to Vermont's Northeast Kingdom, where he practiced primary care medicine at the Hardwick Area Health Center for thirty four years, until his retirement in 2019.

He continues to live in East Hardwick with his wife Helen, a retired school psychologist. Their children, Matthew and Emma, live in California and Utah

RESEARCH SOURCES and BIBLIOGRAPHY

Articles/Books/Magazines/Websites

Barsch, Sky. *Vermont Sports*, December 26, 2009.

Burns, Adam. "Vermont Railroads in The Green Mountain State." American-Rails, 2002 (www.american-rails.com).

Dow, Wiz. "Hardwick on the Map, 1895-1915." Masters Thesis, University of Vermont, 1985.

History of the Bardwell Hotel, a booklet published by the Rutland Historical Society.

Jacobson, Adam. *Radio+Television Business Report*, June 21, 2017.

Lake Champlain Land Trust, website (www.lclt.org).

Sabin, James, et. al. *History of Waterbury, Vermont 1915-1991*. Waterbury Historical Society, 1991.

Shinn, Peggy. *International Skiing History Association Magazine*, August 5, 2016.

Walsh, Kevin. "Visit the Ruins of Waterbury's Little River Settlement." Stowe Today, Vermont Community Newspaper Group, June 21, 2010 (www.vtcng.com/stowetoday).

Newspapers

The Burlington Free Press (1976)

The Hardwick Gazette (1994-2015)

The Montpelier Times-Argus (1962-66)

The Montpelier Bridge (2018)

The Rutland Herald (1966-1974)

The Springfield Reporter (1965-66)

Historical Societies/Organizations

Camp Abnaki Archives

Hardwick Historical Society (Wiz Dow)

Patten Free Library

Rutland Historical Society

Waterbury Historical Society

Wyoming (Ohio) Historical Society (Sherry Sheffield)

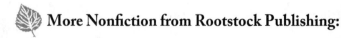 **More Nonfiction from Rootstock Publishing:**

Alzheimer's Canyon: One Couple's Reflections on Living with Dementia by
Jane Dwinell & Sky Yardley

The Atomic Bomb on My Back
by Taniguchi Sumiteru

*Catalysts for Change: How Nonprofits and a Foundation Are Helping Shape
Vermont's Future* ed.
by Doug Wilhelm

China in Another Time: A Personal Story
by Claire Malcolm Lintilhac

Collecting Courage: Joy, Pain, Freedom, Love —
Anti-Black Racism in the Charitable Sector
eds. Nneka Allen, Camila Vital Nunes Pereira, & Nicole Salmon

Cracked: My Life After a Skull Fracture
by Jim Barry

I Could Hardly Keep From Laughing:
An Illustrated Collection of Vermont Humor
by Don Hooper & Bill Mares

A Judge's Odyssey: From Vermont to Russia, Kazakhstan, and Georgia,
Then on to War Crimes and Organ Trafficking in Kosovo
by Dean B. Pineles

The Language of Liberty: A Citizen's Vocabulary
by Edwin C. Hagenstein
A Lawyer's Life to Live
by Kimberly B. Cheney

Lifelines: Antidotes to Animus and Angst
by Bobbie Wayne

Nobody Hitchhikes Anymore
by Ed Griffin-Nolan

Pauli Murray's Revolutionary Life
by Simki Kuznick

Preaching Happiness: Creating a Just and Joyful World
by Ginny Sassaman

*Red Scare in the Green Mountains: Vermont in the
McCarthy Era 1946-1960*
by Rick Winston

Save Me a Seat! A Life with Movies by Rick Winston

*Striding Rough Ice: Coaching College Hockey and
Growing Up in the Game*
by Gary Wright

Tales of Bialystok: A Jewish Journey from Czarist Russia to America
by Charles Zachariah Goldberg

Uncertain Fruit: A Memoir of Infertility, Loss, and Love
by Rebecca & Sallyann Majoya

Walking Home: Trail Stories
by Celia Ryker

You Have a Hammer: Building Grant Proposals for Social Change
by Barbara Floersch

To learn about our Fiction, Poetry, and Children's titles, visit
our website www.rootstockpublishing.com.